A New Owner's
Guide to
PAPILLONS

JG-170

PHOTO CREDITS

Leah Atwood—p. 112
Karen & Steve Baird—pp. 7, 59, 125 & 147
Debi Davis—pp. 5 & 19
Cindy Glass—p. 84
Myrtle Rae Greenwood—p. 145
David Kraft—pp. 71 & 136
Gail Magilke—pp. 5, 22, 28, 64 & 99
Patrick Mondont—pp. 18 & 124
John Oulton—p. 13
Jeff Poling—pp. 67, 109, 140 & 154
Nancy Ridge—pp. 27 & 69
Ben Treichel—pp. 4, 25, 35, 101, 135, 141, 148, 149, 155 & 157
Deborah Wood—pp. 3, 73 & 76

**The photo of Edith Wharton (p. 11) is reprinted by permission of
the Estate of Edith Wharton and the Watkins/Loomis Agency.**

All other photos by Isabelle Francais.

T.F.H. Publications, Inc.
One TFH Plaza
Third and Union Avenues
Neptune City, NJ 07753

This book has been published with the intent to provide accurate and authoritative information in regard to the subject matter within. While every precaution has been taken in preparation of this book, the publisher and author assume no responsibility for errors or omissions. Neither is any liability assumed for damages resulting from the use of the information herein.

ISBN 0-7938-2819-8

www.tfh.com

A New Owner's Guide to
PAPILLONS

Deborah Wood

Contents

2003 Edition

A distinguishing characteristic of the Papillon is the "butterfly wing" ears.

Grooming a Papillon takes time and patience.

His small stature and adorable appearance make the Papillon a favorite among dog fanciers.

A well-trained Papillon will make a great addition to any family.

Papillons make excellent companions and assistance dogs.

His small stature and adorable appearance make the Papillon a favorite among dog fanciers.

HISTORY and Origin of the Papillon

The history of humans is inextricably linked with the history of dogs. When we foraged for game in the earliest days of humankind, our dogs were our partners. When humans made the transition from nomadic hunters to settling down in agricultural communities, we bred dogs to herd our flocks of goats, sheep, and cattle. Guard dogs have protected us from the very dawn of our civilized existence to the present day.

But the intertwined history of humans and dogs is by no means limited to working dogs. Two thousand years ago, small temple dogs in Tibet were providing comfort and inspiration to monks. A thousand years ago, small dogs were already in the courts of Europe. We humans seem to need our companion dogs every bit as much as we need their guarding, herding, and hunting cousins.

The Papillon who is playing in your living room has a rich and regal family history. In fact, your Papillon's ancestors were favorites in the royal courts throughout Europe.

The Papillon is descended from the Continental Toy Spaniel. Drop-eared Papillons (called Phalenes) still look very much like the dogs of the royal courts from hundreds of years ago.

EARLY HISTORY

Papillons are descended from toy-sized spaniels, called Continental Toy Spaniels, that were popular among European royalty since the beginning of the last millenium. Of course, a thousand years ago, no one was writing down the pedigrees of their lap dogs, so the exact history of these toy spaniels will probably always be a mystery.

That doesn't stop canine historians from arguing, of course. Some historians will tell you with absolute certainty that small dogs from Asia (such as Japanese Chin and Tibetan Spaniels) were the ancestors of the toy dogs of Europe. These historians contend that small Asian dogs that were brought to Europe by early adventurers were cross-bred with European spaniels, creating lap-sized spaniels that made popular royal pets.

Others heartily disagree. They argue that the miniaturization of spaniel breeds in Europe could easily have happened when the favorite, small lap dogs were bred with other beloved small pet dogs, without any cross-breeding with dogs from Asia.

We'll never know for sure what dogs were bred together to create the early court dogs, but by as early as the 1200s, there were dogs throughout the royal houses of Europe that were identifiable as Continental Toy Spaniels. These little spaniels varied in size and substance and are the ancestors of today's Papillons, Cavalier King Charles Spaniels, and English Toy Spaniels.

CONTINENTAL TOY SPANIELS IN THE PAINTINGS OF THE MASTERS

One of the joys of owning a dog with such a distinguished heritage is looking at the paintings of these dogs throughout history. The first painting with a Papillon-like dog dates back to the 1200s. It's amazing to think that in the age of chivalrous knights and the great Crusades, the ancestors of our dogs were playing in medieval courtyards.

Just as our family photos wouldn't be complete without our dogs, a royal painting of the Renaissance apparently wasn't complete without a Continental Toy Spaniel. By the 1400s and early 1500s, a surprising number of paintings contained images of small, particolored, drop-eared, dainty little dogs.

Great painters, including Titian, Rubens, Watteau, Van Dyke, Velaquez, and Toulouse-Latrec all painted portraits that included

Papillon-like dogs. One of the most beautiful paintings is one called *Louis XIV and Family,* by Largille. It shows the King Louis XIV (who ruled France from 1643 to 1715), with several family members—including a little girl and a lively little black and white dog. The dog is giving a happy play bow to the child. The fine-boned structure, plumed tail, and blaze down the face make this dog look very much like a modern-day Phalene (drop-eared Papillon).

THE ROYAL DOGS OF FRANCE

The Continental Toy Spaniel was especially coveted in the royal palaces of France. There are many stories about the importance

As delicate as a porcelain figurine, the Papillon has captured the hearts of owners in homes around the world.

of our Papillons' ancestors in the lives of their royal masters.

The strangest tale is the life and death story of King Henry III of France. He reigned in a time of deep religious strife, an eccentric monarch who apparently often carried baskets of Toy Spaniels around his neck—including when he appeared before his Council of State. There is a report that one of his dogs expressed great dislike for a monk who came to deliver a letter. The monk turned out to be a fanatical Dominican friar named Jacque Clement, who stabbed the king on August 1, 1589. Henry III died the following day.

Madame Pompadour (who lived from 1721 to 1764) was the powerful mistress to Louis XV. She had two Papillons, Inez and Mimi. It's stunning that few people's names survive down to us from 300 years ago, but the names of Madame Pompadour's dogs are still on the lips of Papillon lovers.

The most famous person to own one of the early ancestors of the Papillon was Marie Antoinette. There is even a small statue that was saved from her royal palace that looks a little bit like a Papillon (although it has quite round eyes, so it also looks a little like a Japanese Chin or a Pekingese). There is a colorful legend (which is almost certainly not true) that Marie Antoinette's faithful Papillon hid under her skirts and accompanied her to the guillotine. One version of the legend says that her executioner kept the dog until the end of the dog's days.

BUTTERFLY EARS

Over time, Papillons grew to be distinguished from the other European lap dogs. Papillons are smaller, daintier, and more delicate than the other dogs that descended from the Continental Toy Spaniel.

And, of course, no other breed has those amazing ears. Papillon (usually pronounced *PAP-ee-yawn*) is the French word for butterfly—because Papillon ears look amazingly like butterfly wings. These distinctive, upright, butterfly ears were primarily developed during the late 1800s and early 1900s. At about this time, the term "Papillon" began to be widely used as the breed name.

The most notable feature of the Papillon is the butterfly ears.

Much more recently, around the 1940s, the term "Phalene," a French word for "moth," was coined for the drop-eared variety of Papillon. ("Phalene" is usually pronounced *FAY-leen* or *fah-LEN*.) The ears of a Phalene are supposed to resemble the closed wings of a moth, while the ears of the erect-eared Papillon are supposed to resemble the outstretched wings of a butterfly.

Novelist Edith Wharton was one of America's earliest fanciers of Papillons. Here the famed author is pictured with two old-fashioned Paps in 1890.

PAPILLONS IN THE UNITED STATES

Papillons came to the United States at the turn of the 20th century. Novelist Edith Wharton, the first woman to earn a Pulitzer prize, was one of the very first Americans to own a Papillon. When Wharton wrote these wonderful words in *In Provence and Lyrical Epigrams,* "she was probably describing one of her beloved Papillons.

> *"My little old dog:*
> *A heart-beat*
> *At my feet."*

Papillons were recognized by the American Kennel Club (AKC) in 1915. A dog named Joujou became the first champion Papillon that year. Most of the early American Papillons were imported from England, France, and Belgium.

The Papillon Club of America (PCA) formed in 1935. Today, the PCA is an active breed club, holding the National Papillon Specialty Show each year. The PCA also oversees Papillon rescue, keeps historic records, and provides information about Papillons to beginning pet owners and knowledgeable exhibitors alike.

For decades, Papillons were considered great little dogs for people who were "in the know." Relatively rare, with fewer than a thousand dogs registered in a year, these dogs were usually owned by people who had done a lot of research into dog breeds and were looking for a lively, intelligent, thinking companion in a small package. If you walked a Papillon down the street, people would stop and ask all kinds of questions, because most people outside of the dog show world had never seen this little dog with the enormous ears.

History in the Making

The past decade has probably been the most important in the centuries-long history of the breed. It all started with one dog: Ch. Loteki Supernatural Being—known to his millions of fans as Kirby.

In 1999, Kirby won Best in Show at the Westminster Kennel Club dog show. This event—the "superbowl of dog shows"—attracts millions of television viewers.

Kirby's elegant looks and big dog personality charmed millions of viewers who watched the event on television, and certainly made the breed more recognizable to the general public than ever before. After Kirby won Westminster, breeders were inundated with calls from people who wanted to own a Papillon. Many newcomers to

Ch. Loteki Supernatural Being won Best in Show at the 1999 Westminster Kennel Club dog show in New York. This win, viewed by millions of television viewers, has helped to increase the popularity of the Papillon.

the breed were first inspired to learn more about Papillons when they saw Kirby beating the big dogs with so much style and confidence.

Suddenly, this relatively unknown breed was in the spotlight and nothing has been the same since. In just a few years, the number of Papillons registered with the AKC has doubled—and if the trend continues, will double again soon. For the first time in its history with the AKC, Papillons are ranked in the top 40 most popular breeds and are expected to continue to increase in popularity.

Popularity for any breed brings potential dangers. To date, the vast majority of Papillon breeders have been people who have zealously guarded the health, intelligence, and vitality of this special breed. People who care deeply about the breed are now working hard to educate the general public about these little dogs and about the importance of buying from a reputable breeder.

As a new Papillon owner, you can be part of this effort. Explain the importance of getting a dog from a breeder who socializes her dogs and who breeds dogs that look and act like the dog described in the Papillon breed standard. Your efforts to educate the public and to be a responsible owner will help preserve the future of our wonderful little dogs.

Papillons have an illustrious and fabled past. The future of these dogs is in the hands of the people who own them today.

CHARACTERISTICS of the Papillon

A Real Dog in Disguise

This little dog is graceful and dainty in his appearance. With an appealing face framed by butterfly-like ears, a Papillon looks more like an adorable stuffed animal than a dog. But these busy, athletic, energetic, cheerful, intelligent dogs don't fit the stereotype of little lap dogs. There is probably no accomplishment in the world of dogs that a Papillon hasn't achieved. They work as loyal service dogs to people with disabilities, and some of the top obedience dogs in the country have been Papillons. They also excel at the physically demanding sports of agility and flyball.

Papillons are energetic, busy, curious, bright little dogs. For those of us who love them, there is no more wonderful breed in the world. Still, like any other breed of dog, Papillons aren't for everyone. The same traits that some people find endearing, other people find hard to live with.

The Papillon's ears with their fringes are one of the things that people comment about when they first are introduced to this breed.

THOSE AMAZING EARS

The first thing that people notice about Papillons are those amazing ears. No other breed has such large ears that stick up—giving the Papillon a look of perpetual alertness and surprise.

Ear fringes—flowing hair that grows along the edges of the ears—are prized. These fringes add the appearance of size of the ears, making the dogs look more than ever like they're wearing hairy little butterfly masks.

Watch your Papillon's ears and you'll notice that not only do they look like butterfly wings, but they also move like butterfly wings. They're remarkably mobile, and one ear will often move quite independently of the other. "Yoda," "Gizmo," "Angel," and "Radar" are common Papillon names, because of those amazing ears.

Phalenes

Although most people think of Papillons as having those huge, erect, butterfly ears, it's also perfectly normal for Papillons to have drop ears. These dogs are called Phalenes, a French word for moth.

Phalenes look very much like many of the original Continental Toy Spaniels in the paintings of the masters, and there is a keen interest among serious Papillon fanciers in keeping the Phalene in the public eye and part of breeding programs.

The drop ears change the Papillon expression dramatically, making the dogs appear much softer. Rest assured, there is no difference in the personalities of drop-eared Phalenes and their erect-eared counterparts. Phalenes and erect-eared Papillons are bred together and occur in the same litter.

A RAINBOW OF COLORS

Papillons are basically white dogs with markings of practically any color you see in dogdom: coppery reds, shimmering blacks, all shades of sable, and even lemon. The colors come in all kinds of combinations.

Show dogs don't have any white on their ears (the dark ears looking more like butterfly wings). Ideally, they also have a white blaze down their face, looking like the body of the butterfly.

LITTLE CANINE EINSTEINS

Although most people are first drawn to Papillons because of the breed's appearance, it doesn't take long to realize that what really

Papillons are white dogs with markings of practically any color. They have a white blaze down the front of the face that resembles the butterfly's body when matched with the ear "wings."

sets Papillons apart from other breeds is their personalities. It isn't a coincidence that Papillons are among the most successful breeds in all of dogdom in obedience and agility competitions. Most Papillons are intelligent, problem-solving, active little dogs.

Many Papillons—and their owners—face heartache when people confuse the dog's adorable outward appearance with the personality of the dog underneath the fur. If you want a quiet lap dog who enjoys nothing more than spending the day snuggled up on a couch calmly watching television with you, then another breed is probably a better choice. If you're looking for a fun-loving, adventurous dog who likes to learn tricks, wants to go wherever you do, and loves to play games, a Papillon just might fill the bill.

Papillons love to learn—and enjoy a challenge. Talk with Papillon owners and you'll hear stories of dogs who learned to open kitchen cabinets to get a favorite toy or treat. It's common for Papillons to trick other dogs out of toys by running to the door and barking wildly—when the other dog drops her toy to see what the commotion is about, the first one will neatly turn and grab the abandoned toy.

FIRST-CLASS ATHLETES

Papillons excel at canine sports. They earn more obedience, agility, and tracking titles each year than many other toy breeds *combined.*

Paps have participated in obedience trials and agility competitions with much success. They are responsible for more titles in dog sports than many other toy breeds combined.

Papillons have been competing in obedience trials in the United States for nearly 50 years. Advanced obedience competition requires a dog to do complex tasks, including obeying hand signals, finding articles just by scent, retrieving a dumbbell over a high jump ("high" possibly meaning 10 inches for a Papillon), and staying in a "sit" for 3 minutes and a "down" for 5 minutes in a line of strange dogs while the handlers leave the building. Papillons are one of the premiere obedience breeds and by far the best tiny obedience breed.

These dainty-looking dogs with the butterfly ears have been stars in agility competition since the sport became popular in the last decade. Agility is basically a timed run through an obstacle course—dogs fly over hurdles, slither through above-ground tunnels, climb over A-frames, tiptoe across dogwalks (doggie balance beams five feet in the air), and slalom through weave poles. The top dogs do this at a dead run. In 1999, the AKC added the title of Master Agility Champion (MACH)—and 3 of the first 16 dogs of all breeds to earn this demanding, prestigious, new title were Papillons. Many Papillons have also earned tracking titles, in which dogs follow a scent trail to find the path a person walked.

In fact, the first dog of *any* breed to receive top honors in conformation, obedience, tracking, and agility is a Papillon, OTCh. Ch. Loteki Sudden Impulse UDX TDX MX (called "Zack"). The "Ch." in front of Zack's name indicates that he earned the title of Champion for his beauty in the show ring. OTCh. (Obedience Trial Champion) and UDX (Utility Dog Excellent) are titles that demonstrate he's a top obedience dog. TDX (Tracking Dog Excellent) is earned by following a trail at least 1,000 feet, over obstacles, around turns, and across intersecting scent trails. The MX was the top agility title at the time Zack was competing. Multi-titled dogs like Zack are proof that Papillons have it all: brains, beauty, athleticism, and instinct, all in a small body.

SERVICE DOGS

Papillons have exceptional intelligence, and several have been called on to work as service dogs, profoundly changing the lives of their humans. In 1999, a Papillon named Peek was named Delta Society's Service Animal of the Year.

Peek's partner, Debi Davis, has vascular disease. As a result, her legs have been amputated and she uses a wheel chair. Davis becomes dizzy when she leans down. Peek helps Davis every day, doing a variety of jobs such as picking up pens, coins, and even newspapers from the floor; pulling the laundry out of the dryer; bringing Davis the phone; helping to make the bed; and opening and shutting drawers, cabinets, and doors. He can turn on and off light switches, press elevator buttons, and even give money to a cashier.

Debi Davis and her Papillon, Peek, enjoy a day out shopping. Peek helps Debi with everyday tasks that are difficult for her, such as picking up items.

THE FLIP SIDE OF THE COIN

While it sounds intriguing to have such a clever, athletic dog, think twice. For humans and dogs alike, their strong points can also be their drawbacks. A dog with enough intelligence and drive to work as a service dog may be too much of a handful to be a content family pet.

Dogs that are great athletes seem to have springs on their toes and seem to spend as much time in the air as a butterfly—or at least Michael Jordan. Some Papillons can leap straight from the ground up four feet into the air. While this athletic enthusiasm is entertaining, it means careful management for your Papillon, especially if he's one who spends much of his life airborne. Some Papillons require a yard with a six-foot fence if they're loose in a yard, or else they can escape.

Although almost all Papillons are lively, people-oriented dogs, there is a range of energy levels and the need for constant entertainment among Papillons. Some Papillons reflect the more laid-back personality of their spaniel ancestors and are content to chase a toy around the living room for 15 minutes and then cuddle contently for an hour. Other Papillons are more like miniature Border Collies, and will generally get themselves into terrible trouble if they don't have at least an hour or two of interactive, demanding activity in a day.

Small Dogs and Small Spaces

One of the great advantages of Papillon ownership is that even the most active Papillon can live happily in a small space. Throw your busy dog's favorite toy across the living room, and she'll break out into a run, leap into the air to snag it, and jump up on the couch to return it to you. Twenty minutes of living room fetch can be a real aerobic workout for a Papillon-sized dog. These dogs can be excellent condo or apartment dogs, because they can get their exercise needs met in a small space.

On the other hand, Papillons can also thrive in country living. They love a romp outside, they're great hiking companions, and they are ecstatic about a walk on the beach. Overall, they're hardy, adaptable little dogs that can adjust to a wide variety of lifestyles.

However, Papillons should never, ever be considered an outside dog. A doghouse isn't nearly enough protection to keep their little bodies safe from the elements. Papillons enjoy the outdoors, but just to visit—they sure don't want to live there permanently!

Small dogs, such as the Papillon, don't need lots of room and can thrive in small places, such as a small apartment.

Sensitive Souls

While Papillons are busy, generally hardy, and certainly athletic dogs, they are also very sensitive dogs. After all, this breed has had a thousand years to perfect its relationship with humans.

Be prepared to spend the next 15 years or more of your life with two bright, brown eyes staring at you, waiting for you to play. Papillons have been bred to be companion dogs for centuries, and they've perfected the art. They'll gaze at you for hours at a time, hoping to lure you into a game of fetch, a walk, a tummy scratch, or other doggie activities. Don't expect to spend a waking minute alone again: not when you're cooking dinner, not when you're reading a book, not even when you're in the bathroom. Papillons are only truly happy when they are with the people they love.

Papillons are exceptionally alert and can be high-strung, but some Papillons are shy. Be aware of this tendency in the breed and think about whether you can provide the calm, quiet, structured household that a shy dog needs to gain confidence and blossom. If a shy, cautious, or "soft" dog isn't for you, be careful when you select your Papillon.

Some Paps are very high-strung while others are shy. Keep this in mind when making your selection.

Adolescent Papillons go through an awkward stage for a few months before reaching their full adult proportions and elegance.

On the other end of the spectrum, some Papillons are very pushy, described by the late dog writer Roger Caras as "little tyrants." These bold, quick, smart dogs can decide that they're far more clever than the humans who inhabit the household and can even nip people who aren't following the dog's orders quickly enough. Both shyness and pushy behaviors can be dealt with by providing structure and gentle training for your dog.

While some Papillons seldom bark, many seem to have a lot to say. Combine this canine gift for gab with hyper-acute hearing and extreme alertness, and you'll find yourself forewarned of people passing by your house, a squirrel scrambling along the fence, the cat in the neighbor's yard, and every bird flying overhead.

Happily, Papillons are easy to train. The best way to deal with a barker is to thank him. After he's barked two or three times, tell him "thank you," and maybe give him a treat. Soon, he'll bark the alarm (which can be useful if you want to know there's a stranger at the door) and come get you for his reward for letting you know.

The Papillon is not necessarily a cuddle-bunny. What could look more cuddly than an adorable Papillon? Many first-time Papillon owners are shocked when their dog would prefer not to snuggle.

While there are many Paps who love nothing better than to nestle in their human's arms, there are more who would prefer to lie nearby and look at their human with adoration. If you're envisioning a dog who loves to cuddle, another breed might be better for you—or choose your Papillon very carefully.

Terrible Teens

It happens all the time with new Papillon owners: They bring home an adorable, fluffy, pretty puppy that looks like a perfect Papillon in miniature. Then, at about four months old, everything changes.

Adolescent Papillons are among the oddest-looking creatures in the world. They shed that cute, fuzzy baby fur, and what looks like the coat of a short-haired dog comes in. When they're teething, Papillons' ears fall up and down, and sometimes even flop over backwards. Sometimes their curly little tails straighten out.

Don't panic: Your puppy will grow out of this stage. His short coat will gradually grow longer. His tail almost surely will gently curve over his back, giving him the correct Papillon appearance.

This stage lasts from about four months of age to ten months of age. After that time, Papillons begin to acquire their elegant coat and adult proportions that will last them for the rest of their lives.

SMALL CHILDREN AND DELICATE DOGS

Very young children and tiny, fine-boned dogs are a bad combination. Children under the age of about seven usually can't fully distinguish between a stuffed animal and a live dog. Even a loving, well-behaved small child might hug, chase, or carry a Papillon in ways that can injure the dog. Children, and adults for that matter, should play with a Papillon puppy while sitting on the floor. Papillon puppies have very delicate little bones, and many young dogs have broken their legs when they decided to take a flying leap from the arms of a standing person.

Although Papillons are usually not aggressive, it's possible that any small dog—including a Papillon—will reach up and bite a child who is squeezing the dog. If you have very small children, look for a larger, sturdier breed. Your child will have a better time playing with the sturdy dog, and the larger breed will enjoy your child in return.

Children and Papillons can become the best of friends as long as both know the rules. Children should play gently with their new dog to prevent injury to the child or the dog.

Because very young children and Papillons aren't a good match, many responsible breeders won't sell a dog to a household with small children. Others will do a thorough analysis of the household to determine if the children are mature and well supervised.

On the other hand, older children and Papillons can be a wonderful combination. While most breeders strive for very small dogs (most show dogs weigh under 8 pounds), even careful breeding will occasionally produce a puppy that's well over the 12-inch height maximum in the breed standard; these dogs might weigh 10 or even 15 pounds. If you're looking for a family pet, a dog that is oversized for the show ring can be a hearty, fun-loving companion for gentle children.

Papillons have excelled in organized dog activities with children. For instance, many 4-H groups have great dog programs in which children learn to train and care for dogs, and Papillons have been a popular breed. AKC dog shows also include junior showmanship competitions, in which children 10 to 18 years of age are judged on how well they present their dogs. Many juniors compete with their Papillons, because the little dogs are trainable and easily controlled by young handlers.

However, even terrific kids can have interests that wax and wane. Any family that buys a Papillon (or any other dog) to appease the pleadings of a child should be ready for adults to step in and take care of the dog. Someone once said that every boy needs a dog — and a mother to take care of it. For the sake of the dog, every child needs a responsible adult who will be sure that all the dog's needs are met if a child ends up less than perfectly responsible.

PAPILLONS AND OTHER CREATURES GREAT AND SMALL

Sadly, big dogs are a serious threat to the safety—and the lives—of our little dogs. Many dogs seem to view Papillons as prey. Perhaps because of a Papillon's small size, quick movements, and generally non-aggressive attitude, a lot of dogs respond to Papillons as they would respond to a rabbit. Although the dangers of sighthounds bred to hunt rabbits (such as Greyhounds or Borzois) and breeds that tend to be dominant with other dogs (such as Rottweilers or Akitas) may be obvious, don't forget that terriers were bred to hunt game far larger than a typical Papillon.

Large dogs can cause serious injury to your Papillon. Supervise all play with a larger dog or restrict play to other small dogs and other Paps.

Because of their small size, the Papillon is prone to injury and broken bones. This little Pap is wearing an Elizabethan collar so as to not cause further injury to his broken leg.

Some Papillon lovers have begun organizing Papillon play days. This allows their dogs to socialize with each other while the owners share stories or important information pertaining to the breed.

Even a sweet, friendly, large dog isn't a suitable playmate for a Papillon. Dogs play by placing paws on each other's backs and by bumping each other with their bodies. One friendly swipe from a large dog's paw can break your Papillon's slender spine.

Of course, there are many wonderful large dogs and dogs with high prey drives that would never harm your Papillon. However, your little dog relies on you for his safety and his life. It takes only one fateful second for your dog to be crushed by the jaws or paws of another dog.

If your Papillon shares a home with a large dog, be very careful about their interactions. Normal dog dominance behavior, such as a snap when the other dog comes close to a favorite resting spot or a body block to claim a toy, can be fatal to your Papillon. Some households keep large and small dogs in separate rooms. Others allow supervised peaceful co-existence, as long as everyone behaves.

Papillons should never be left loose in the house with a larger dog when the humans are gone. You are asking to come home

Most Papillon owners soon realize that just one Pap is not enough. Getting a playmate for your older dog will help to keep him out of trouble when you're away.

to a tragedy. This is not extreme if you've spent a few years around people who have owned Papillons. Almost everyone knows a Papillon that has been grievously wounded or even killed by a large dog that decided to hunt, attack, or just play. Small dogs like Papillons should never play with large dogs—ever.

Papillons usually get along famously with other small dogs and enjoy energetic games of tag with appropriately-sized best friends. Try to find opportunities for play dates with other small dogs.

Papillons take special pleasure in playing with other Papillons. There are few more delightful sights in the world that a flock of

When visiting a breeder, her Papillons should look healthy and loved. They should not shy away from people.

butterfly dogs leaping, feinting, running, and chasing each other. These energetic games can last for hours, leaving all dogs happily tired at the end of the day.

Some Papillon lovers have begun organizing Papillon play days. This is a great opportunity for Papillons to play with each other, and for the humans to share stories and suggestions about the dogs they love.

Papillons usually get along well with other small animals. Many cats and Papillons have become the best of friends, playing happily, grooming each other, and joining in the hunt for any insect that dares to find itself in the house. But give the cat plenty of space to call her own and introduce cats and dogs gradually. Their friendship will strengthen over time.

Many Papillons have also become buddies with budgies, rabbits, and even mice. However, keep a close eye on interactions with other species. Papillons often have a very high prey drive, especially around birds and small rodents. If you want a long-lived friendship, be sure your Papillon is on his best behavior!

It's Like the Potato Chip Ad...

It doesn't take most Papillon owners long to realize something: They don't want just one. Papillons are generally compatible little dogs and enjoy a best friend. They entertain each other, and most will play endless games of tag, tug, and zoomies.

Because most Papillons aren't aggressive with other dogs, two males or two females usually get along well. If you have a very pushy dog of either gender, you might consider getting a Papillon of the opposite sex to avoid squabbles.

Although two Papillons can be easier, and even more entertaining, than one, *don't get two puppies at the same time!* Papillons can be difficult to housetrain, and two puppies at the same time can be nearly impossible. Plus, the puppies may bond so tightly to one another that there isn't much room for the humans in their lives. Wait until your first Papillon is at least a year old before adding the new puppy.

How you treat interactions during the first few days may determine whether the two dogs become mortal enemies or best friends.

Here are some tips:

The worst mistake an owner can make is to bring the new dog

right into the house. The newcomer has just waltzed into your existing dog's territory. It's best to take both dogs for a walk and let them decide they like each other on neutral turf.

If they're buddies—or at least tolerate one another—in a neutral place, then the two dogs are likely to have a good relationship when they come home together.

A good rule of thumb is to give the existing dog 75 percent of the attention for the first 2 weeks. The last thing you want to do is have the older dog feel left out and jealous of the new dog. If you do this, you'll see your older dog visibly relax after several days, and you can begin giving both dogs equal attention.

Remind your older dog of his importance by walking him first, feeding him first, and spending special time alone together.

Most Papillons become deeply devoted to the new dog in the family right away. Two dogs really can be twice the fun of having just one. If there's room in your heart, and in your house, for a second busy, clever, adventurous, little dog, it can be a great joy.

Whether you have one Papillon or a whole flock of butterfly dogs, your life will never be the same. These thinking, active, demanding, intelligent dogs are unique in dogdom and a source of constant joy if they're matched with the right human.

STANDARD of the Papillon

Every breed has a standard—a blueprint that describes the height, weight, color, head, tail, and even toes of the breed. At dog shows, every dog is judged on how well he or she conforms to the standard (that's why dog show competition is called *conformation*.) Just as no human is a "perfect ten," no dog perfectly meets the standard for any breed. Certainly, a Papillon that doesn't even come close to being a show dog can still be a fabulous pet.

So why should someone who just wants a pet pay attention to the standard? The standard defines, physically and temperamentally, what makes a Papillon different from every other breed of dog. Breeders who use the standard as their guide will create Papillons that retain the healthy structure, wonderful temperament, and unique appearance that draws us to these remarkable dogs.

Breed standards vary from country to country and from registry to registry. Become familiar with the standard that applies to your area.

The Papillon is a small, friendly, elegant toy dog of fine-boned structure. He should be light, dainty, and of lively action.

One of the advantages of owning a purebred dog is that we can be pretty sure how our dogs will grow up to look and act . It is the guidelines created by the standard that give purebred dogs their relative uniformity across the nation and even around the world.

Even if you would never dream of owning a show dog and if you never go to a dog show, purchase your dog or puppy from a breeder who cares about breeding to the standard. With the stewardship of ethical breeders and responsible owners, our dogs can expect to remain the bright, athletic, beautiful dogs that they are today.

THE OFFICIAL AKC BREED STANDARD FOR THE PAPILLON

General Appearance—The Papillon is a small, friendly, elegant toy dog of fine-boned structure, light, dainty and of lively action; distinguished from other breeds by its beautiful butterfly-like ears.

Size, Proportion, Substance—*Size*—Height at withers, 8 to 11 inches. *Fault*—Over 11 inches. *Disqualification*—Over 12 inches. *Proportion*—Body must be slightly longer than the height at withers. It is not a cobby dog. Weight is in proportion to height. *Substance*—Of fine-boned structure.

Head—*Eyes* dark, round, not bulging, of medium size and alert in *expression*. The inner corners of the eyes are on line with the stop.

Eye rims black. *Ears*—The ears of either the erect or drop type should be large with rounded tips, and set on the sides and toward the back of the head. (1) Ears of the erect type are carried obliquely and move like the spread wings of a butterfly. When alert, each ear forms an angle of approximately 45 degrees to the head. The leather should be of sufficient strength to maintain the erect position. (2) Ears of the drop type, known as the Phalene, are similar to the erect type, but are carried drooping and must be completely down. *Faults*—Ears small, pointed, set too high; one ear up, or ears partly down.

The ears are carried obliquely and move like the spread wings of a butterfly. When alert, the ears should form a 45-degree angle to the head.

Skull—The head is small. The skull is of medium width and slightly rounded between the ears. A well-defined stop is formed where the muzzle joins the skull. *Muzzle*—The muzzle is fine, abruptly thinner than the head, tapering to the nose. The length of the muzzle from the tip of the nose to stop is approximately one-third the length of the head from tip of nose to occiput. *Nose* black, small, rounded and slightly flat on top. *The following fault shall be severely penalized*—Nose not black. *Lips* tight, thin and black. Tongue must not be visible when jaws are closed. *Bite*—Teeth must meet in a scissors bite. *Faults*—Overshot or undershot.

Neck, Topline, Body—*Neck* of medium length. *Topline*—The backline is straight and level. *Body*—The chest is of medium depth with ribs well sprung. The belly is tucked up. *Tail* long, set high and carried well arched over the body. The tail is covered with a long, flowing plume. The plume may hang to either side of the body.

The Papillon's head should be small with the skull being of medium width and slightly rounded between the ears. The muzzle is fine, abruptly thinner than the head, tapering to the nose.

A variety of colors is acceptable in the Papillon. An all white dog or a dog with no white at all is to be severely penalized.

Faults—Low-set tail; one not arched over the back, or too short.

Forequarters—Shoulders well developed and laid back to allow freedom of movement. Forelegs slender, fine-boned and must be straight. Removal of dewclaws on forelegs optional. Front feet thin and elongated (hare-like), pointing neither in nor out.

Hindquarters—Well developed and well angulated. The hind legs are slender, fine-boned, and parallel when viewed from behind. Hocks inclined neither in nor out. Dewclaws, if any, must be removed from hind legs. Hind feet thin and elongated (hare-like), pointing neither in nor out.

Coat—Abundant, long, fine, silky, flowing, straight with resilient quality, flat on back and sides of body. A profuse frill on chest. There is no undercoat. Hair short and close on skull, muzzle, front of forelegs, and from hind feet to hocks. Ears well fringed, with the inside covered with silken hair of medium length. Backs of the forelegs are covered with feathers diminishing to the pasterns. Hind legs are covered to the hocks with abundant breeches (culottes). Tail is covered with a long, flowing plume. Hair on feet is short, but fine tufts may appear over toes and grow beyond them, forming a point.

Color—Always parti-color or white with patches of any color(s). On the head, color(s) other than white must cover both ears, back and front, and extend without interruption from the ears over both eyes. A clearly defined white blaze and noseband are preferred to a solidly marked head. Symmetry of facial markings is desirable. The size, shape, placement, and presence or absence of patches of color on the body are without importance. Among the colors there is no preference, provided nose, eye rims and lips are well pigmented black.

The following faults shall be severely penalized—Color other than white not covering both ears, back and front, or not extending from the ears over both eyes. A slight extension of the white collar onto the base of the ears, or a few white hairs interspersed among the color, shall not be penalized, provided the butterfly appearance is not sacrificed.

Disqualifications—An all white dog or a dog with no white.

Gait—Free, quick, easy, graceful, not paddlefooted, or stiff in hip movements.

Temperament—Happy, alert and friendly. Neither shy nor aggressive.

DISQUALIFICATIONS
Height over 12 inches.
An all white dog or a dog with no white.
Approved June 10, 1991
Effective July 31, 1991

SELECTING the Right Papillon for You

You've made the decision: A Papillon is for you. You're ready to go out and get your new dog. Sorry, it's not that easy. Especially with the rising popularity of the breed, demand is outpacing supply. In the past, the breed was almost exclusively in the hands of a small cadre of dedicated hobby breeders. With rising popularity, unfortunately, has come a small tidal wave of new breeders—some responsible and some decidedly not.

The first few weeks in your dog's life are the most important: what happens during that time will hugely affect your dog's long-term health, her ability to accept new situations and new people, her attitude toward other dogs, and even her ability to learn and think.

Scientists have identified *critical periods* in puppy development. They've proved that puppies with confident, nurturing mothers; varied, appropriate experiences in new places; and certain kinds of interaction with humans grow up to be healthier, smarter, and happier than puppies that don't have those experiences.

Papillon puppies are absolutely adorable. Take your time and examine a number of pups before making your final selection.

RESPONSIBLE BREEDERS

If you want a great dog, get your Papillon puppy from a great breeder. This person must be knowledgeable about puppy development and be committed to the welfare of the breed and to the well being of her dogs.

When you go to look at puppies, first and foremost, use common sense. Here are things to consider:

- Are the dogs well cared for? Are the puppies and their mother (and any other dogs who live there) clean? Are they happy and friendly with the breeder and with strangers?
- Do the dogs who live there have a good life? That means living inside, with access to outside play areas that are clean and healthy. Too many breeders raise Papillons in small cages, 24 hours a day. While sleeping in crates at bedtime, and keeping females in heat separate from males, are good, ethical practices, keeping animals confined in small cages all day is cruel.
- Do you want this person breeding more dogs? It's easy to feel sorry for a puppy and decide to "rescue" him from a sad situation. Unfortunately, all you've accomplished is to line the pocket of an unethical breeder. If she makes money on a litter, she will just breed another (and another.) Don't give your money to anyone whose dogs live in unhappy, unclean, unpleasant conditions. There are responsible Papillon breeders, so support the people who raise puppies with love and care. Anything else merely supports a cycle of abuse and neglect for these wonderful little dogs.

Warning Signs

There are warning signs that are a tip-off that you're not working with an ethical breeder. Think twice, and then again, before buying a dog if:

- The parents aren't AKC registered, and the puppies don't have a litter registration. The AKC has minimal health and record-keeping standards for high-volume breeders. If the puppies you're looking at aren't registered, there's a good chance this breeder failed those simple standards. Be especially leery of dogs who are registered in another organization instead of the AKC. When the AKC established minimum standards for large breeders, some of the worst breeders created their own "kennel clubs" so they could tell unsuspecting, naïve buyers that the dogs were

Don't neglect your old dog when bringing a new dog into the home. Spend plenty of time with your existing dog so that he still knows that he is loved.

Ask lots of questions of the breeder when visiting her kennel. Also be prepared to answer some questions, too.

"registered." The bottom line should be: no AKC registration, no sale.

- The breeder suggests meeting you someplace other than her home. A good breeder should be proud of the sparkling clean, happy place her puppies live. She wouldn't dream of meeting someone at a park or a freeway rest stop to sell a puppy.
- She sells puppies before they are 12 weeks old. Papillons puppies are tiny. For health and safety reasons, good breeders keep them until they are at least 12 weeks old, with very, very rare exception. Be suspicious of anyone who is selling Papillon puppies younger than 12 weeks old.
- The breeder is reluctant for you to meet her other dogs. A good breeder is thrilled with her contributions to the world of dogs. If she is hesitant for you to meet her other dogs, this is a signal that something is wrong.
- The breeder has too many dogs or has dogs of several breeds. Serious breeders usually limit their breeding to one or two breeds and become true experts in their own breeds. A good hobby breeder may have more dogs than most people, but they never have 50.

With Papillon popularity increasing, it's easy to get frustrated. Some breeders have long waiting lists. It's better to wait a year and get a puppy that's been loved, socialized, and given a great start in life.

Promise yourself—and your new puppy—that you will wait for a kind and loving breeder when you buy your dog. Don't give your money to anyone who doesn't have the best interests of dogs at heart.

Finding a Great Breeder

With just a little effort and some minor homework, you can find the kind of breeder who gives her puppies a great start. Here's where to look:

The Papillon Club of America website. The Papillon Club of America is on the Internet at www.papillonclub.org. It lists breeders who are club members who have agreed to a code of ethics. Of course, you should always check out the breeder personally, but this list is an excellent starting point.

Dog Shows. Another excellent place to look for a breeder is at a local dog show. Talk with the people who are showing their dogs

There are a number of different ways to local a reputable breeder. Consult the Papillon Club of America, check out websites, and ask Papillon owners at dog shows for breeders they recommend.

(when they're not busy), and get a sense of the dogs and the people who impress you. Make an appointment to go visit them or write to them later. Every show has a catalogue for sale that includes the name and mailing address for every exhibitor; this is a great way to contact prospective breeders. While you are at the show, you might want to check to see if there are any Papillons in the obedience or agility competitions that often accompany all-breed shows. These competitors often select dogs based on their temperament and physical soundness, and they may be able to tell you where they bought their dogs.

Internet Lists. There are several Internet chat lists for Papillon fanciers. You can have virtual conversations with Papillon lovers around the world. This can be a good way to become acquainted with the breed, and often breeders participate in the discussion. Some of the top names among Papillon breeders and trainers occasionally share their perspectives online with newcomers to the breed.

Of course, Papillons are like any other subject on the Internet—beware of what people tell you. You may never know whether the person who is giving you his or her opinion is a world-renowned expert or a crackpot. Check out any breeders you meet on the Internet with the same healthy skepticism that you would any other Internet meeting.

Even if it's a long trip, try to visit the breeder. Many breeders claim that dogs are "home bred" or "raised under foot." You're never going to find a breeder who says, "I'm unethical and irresponsible." Anyone can say they're the world's best breeder—it's up to you to explore the truth.

Visiting Breeders

Once you have the names of a couple of breeders, make an appointment to go visit them, without the mission of looking for a specific puppy. See if you like the way the breeder treats her dogs. Get to know the adults' personalities. (Remember: the personality of you puppy will be formed by the combination of his genes and his early upbringing—you see both when you look at the breeder and her dogs.)

Papillons should live inside and given time to play outside in a safe environment when the weather is nice.

The home of even the best breeder can seem a little overwhelming. Think of it as the difference between a small family and someone with eight kids. Life is just more chaotic in larger numbers.

A breeder's dogs are likely to sleep in crates at night (even small dogs like Papillons can fill up their humans' beds pretty quickly), and breeders have to keep intact dogs reasonably separated from each other, so they don't end up with any surprise pregnancies. Still, the difference between a happy, healthy multi-dog household and a place where people are breeding dogs for profit will be abundantly clear.

It doesn't matter whether you agree with the breeder's personal politics, admire her décor, or want to be her best friend (although you might find your best friend—you never know). What does matter is that you respect the way she treats her dogs and that you can communicate well, so if you do get a puppy, you can utilize her wisdom.

Be clear about what you want in a Papillon. Papillons are not a uniform breed. They vary widely in size, physical activity levels, personality, and sociability. Think about what role you want your dog to play in your life before you go looking at puppies.

Talk with the breeder about your lifestyle and what you want in a companion. Do you have children? Do you have rare, fragile antiques in your home? Do you think you might want to compete in agility or obedience? Do you spend the winter RV-ing in the sunbelt, or live in the city, or have a farm?

Expect the breeder to ask you invasive, probing, personal questions. She may even insist on coming to your home for a visit. If a breeder loves her dogs, she won't allow them to go to inappropriate homes. You should welcome these questions. A great breeder knows her dogs' souls, and will help you find the right dog for your circumstances. She can't help you if you don't tell her what you want in a pet, and she certainly can't help you if you aren't honest.

Finding the Right Puppy

The day will finally come, and it's time to look at puppies. Picking your own puppy has to be done with both your heart and your head. This is all made more challenging because Papillons usually have very small litters—one puppy isn't unusual, and most litters have only two or three puppies. Take your time to get to know the prospective puppy.

Finding the right Pap for your family takes time and patience. Examine a number of Papillons before bringing one home.

Some Papillons have very demanding personalities while other are more docile. Decide which personality will fit in with you and your family before making your selection.

Start out with an overall impression of the puppy's physical structure and overall health. Are her eyes bright? Is her coat soft and shiny? Is her energy level good? A Papillon with chronic health problems isn't the best choice for a pet.

Take your time when you see a litter. Before you get too attached to a puppy, you need to continue talking with the breeder. Ask her about the personalities that she's seen emerging in the pups.

Ask the breeder about socialization. Some breeders say that their puppies have been well-socialized (and might even believe it) while their puppies have merely lived in an exercise pen in the kitchen.

By the time they're ready to go to new homes (which is 12 weeks of age or older for a small dog like a Papillon), the puppies should have been handled by people of all ages, including children. They should have been exposed to a variety of floor surfaces, such as carpet and linoleum. Weather permitting, they should have had the chance to play outside in a safe area. They should have ridden in a car at least once.

Watch the puppies at rest and play. A puppy may seem calm and easygoing, but that might be because she's ready for a nap. It's a good idea to visit the puppy more than once in order to get a feeling for her overall personality.

Take the puppy away from her mom and littermates, into a different room where she doesn't usually spend a lot of time. See how she bonds with you. Talk with her. Offer some toys to her, and see how she responds.

Beware of a puppy who doesn't want to make eye contact with you or avoids you. This puppy might be shy, sick, or in pain. In any event, the puppy isn't bonding with you.

Keep in mind the adult dog you've dreamed about. Here's a tale of two six-week-old litters, bred by the same breeder and born just five days apart. (It's unusual for a good breeder to have multiple litters at once, but it happens occasionally.) One litter had four pups, the other had two.

All six puppies were friendly, healthy and thriving—but they were very different. One litter was full of action. They careened off the walls and chewed the leg of the visitor. One puppy saw a pair of shoes on the stairs and actually made her way up a stair step that was much taller than she was, in pursuit of the shoe. These puppies were leaping over small objects and playing tug of war.

Different dogs have different personalities. Be patient and find a Papillon with the personality that fits you and your lifestyle,

The second litter was full of gentle souls. They played sweetly and were careful not to bite down hard on the visitor's skin. They stayed close to the visitor, while the other litter was off exploring the far reaches of the room.

Which litter has the "right" puppy? If you have an active lifestyle, and maybe want to compete in agility or obedience, a puppy from that high energy, confident litter is for you. If you want a dog who will be content with a quiet life and spend her life just adoring you, pick one of the quieter, easier-to-live-with puppies.

Because Papillons are still a relatively rare breed, it can be hard to find the Papillon of your dreams. Be patient and wait for the one with the personality that fits your household. Don't try to fit a highly energetic dog into a quiet pet home, and don't try to convince yourself that a cautious little dog will suddenly transform into a bold, lightening-fast performance dog.

Keep in mind your dream dog and she will find you. It may happen with the first litter you meet, and it may be the tenth. You'll know it when it happens. Your puppy will choose you, just as much as you choose the puppy. You'll feel the sense of kinship and rapport. You'll feel that you're bonded from that very first meeting. That's your dog.

MALES VERSUS FEMALES

While the personalities of males and females are apparently quite distinct in some breeds, Papillon personalities don't seem to be determined by gender. Some fanciers say that females tend to be more aloof and tend to be "one-person" dogs, while males tend to be friendlier and more cuddly. However, there are certainly plenty of friendly females and lots of males who would prefer not to cuddle, so pick according to the individual dog, not by the gender.

Unless you are seriously committed to breeding good-quality dogs, which is a world of its own, you will be spaying or neutering your new pet. Reputable breeders will require spaying or neutering, and many will spay or neuter before allowing a pet dog to be sold.

Therefore, don't focus on the "plumbing"—just select a dog that has the personality that meshes best with yours.

PET QUALITY VERSUS SHOW QUALITY

If you're buying a "pet quality" puppy or adult from a show breeder, ask why the puppy isn't show quality. Usually, the

Before you select a Papillon, you need to decide whether you want a pet- or show-quality dog.

differences between a gorgeous pet and a show dog are too subtle for most people to notice: The dog's markings aren't quite perfect or the dog is just a bit too large or too small to compete in the ring. Males with just one descended testicle are disqualified from the ring but may be stunningly beautiful in all the parts the public will see!

However, some reasons for choosing not to show a dog can affect the dog's quality as a pet. If a dog is too shy to enjoy showing, he might not be a happy pet in a boisterous household. If his toes face all four directions, he's not a good prospect for demanding sports like advanced obedience or agility.

HEALTH RECORDS, REGISTRATION PAPERS, AND PUPPY CONTRACTS

If you've gone to a good breeder and found your four-footed soulmate, you're almost done. But there are still some important details you need to discuss with the breeder.

Health Records

While the puppy is nursing, he has immunity from most diseases, passed on through his mother's milk. After that time, vaccinations give your puppy his own immunity. Puppies are given a series of vaccinations between the ages of six weeks and four months. Be sure to get the list of vaccinations that your puppy has received to give to your veterinarian so that you can keep your puppy fully immunized.

Registration Papers

The breeder should show you that both of the puppy's parents are AKC registered and that she has a litter registration for the puppies. The litter registration provides a form for each puppy; when that form is sent in to the AKC, the puppy is a registered dog.

The breeder may do one of four things with your puppy's registration:

1. She may give you the litter registration for the puppy. If so, then you name your puppy and send the form in to the AKC. Talk with the breeder to make sure she doesn't have any requirements for the dog's registered name. For example, some breeders ask all dogs in the litter to have the same letter of the alphabet. Others have themes, such as flowers, classical music, or sports cars. Others like a name that refers to a famous parent or grandparent.

The breeder should supply you with registration papers, a pedigree, a health record, and a diet sheet when you purchase your Papillon.

2. She may give you a spay/neuter contract that allows you to get the registration form after your pet has been altered. This practice is increasingly common among good breeders; as soon as you show the breeder that your pup has been spayed or neutered, then you receive the form to send in to the AKC for registration.

3. She may give you a limited registration. This option is also increasingly common. A limited registration allows you to compete in obedience, agility, and other performance sports, and shows that you have a purebred dog. However, you can't compete in conformation shows, and if your dog were to ever have puppies, the puppies could not be registered.

4. She may have already registered the dog. Some breeders like to register all their own puppies. This allows the breeder to name the dog. The breeder would sign the AKC registration papers over to you at the sale (or after spaying or neutering, if that is the agreement).

All of these options are typical of a reputable breeder. Make sure you understand your agreement with the breeder, and ask questions. **Don't** buy a puppy from a breeder who doesn't have AKC papers on both parents and a litter registration for the puppies. **Don't** buy from a breeder who gives vague promises to get you the papers at some later time. These are red flags that something is wrong.

Pedigree

The pedigree is your pup's family tree. It usually traces your puppy's ancestors back for four or five generations. You might not care much about what famous names are on your dog's pedigree, but it's important to buy from a breeder who cares deeply about genetics and protecting the health, brains, and beauty of the breed. You want to buy from the kind of breeder who is eager and proud to give you a copy of your dog's illustrious lineage. Over time, you also might become more interested in the breed, and it's fun to compare your dog's ancestors with some of the famous dogs that are winning in conformation, obedience, or agility competitions.

Contract

Contracts are very common among good Papillon breeders. If you agree to a contract, read it carefully and understand what you are signing.

Read all contracts carefully. Ultimately, the contract should be written with the long-term well being of the puppy in mind.

Most contracts are written with the long-term well being of the puppy in mind. For example, the contract may require you to spay or neuter your puppy before you can receive your AKC papers. It will probably require you to return the puppy to the breeder if you decide not to keep the puppy—a step that responsible breeders take to ensure their puppies don't later end up in shelters. The contract is also likely to contain health guarantees. Understand what you are agreeing to and be sure you feel comfortable with the arrangement.

Feeding Instructions
If your puppy is younger than six months of age, she's probably eating three times a day. Be sure to get a feeding schedule from your breeder and find out what kind of food your puppy is eating. You'll want to keep the puppy eating the same food on the same schedule, at least for the first week or two.

Puppy Buyer Checklist
• The puppy's parents are AKC registered, and the breeder will supply a registration form, limited registration, or agreement to register the puppy after spay/neuter is complete.

The breeder has provided a copy of the puppy's pedigree.
If there is a contract, you've read it and understand it.

- The puppy has started her vaccinations, and a schedule is included to give to your veterinarian.
- You have discussed the puppy's diet and have food ready for the puppy (either provided by the breeder or purchased before picking up the puppy).
- You have the breeder's phone number in case you have any questions or problems.

Happiness Is a Warm Adult Dog

When most people think about getting a dog, they usually assume they'll be bringing home a puppy. Frankly, puppies can be overrated. There's housetraining, chewing, teething—it's not all fun.

Papillons are, happily, among the healthiest and longest-lived of all breeds. Consider getting an adult instead of a puppy. You won't regret it.

A rescuer who sings the praises of bringing home an older dog says, "You can become so bonded to an older dog you'll swear you gave birth to her." Puppies are adorable, fun, and endearing, but they also take round-the-clock attention. The eventual size, and even the personality, can be hard to judge in a young puppy. Unless you're home full-time, seriously consider taking an older dog.

Many breeders have "change of career" dogs that make great pets. The dog may be a 12-month-old teenager that was kept as a show prospect but didn't quite materialize into a top winner. She might be a retired champion or a brood bitch who has had a few litters and wants to be somebody's "only dog." A breeder should provide registration for an older dog, just as she would a puppy.

Adult Papillons usually adjust very quickly to loving new homes, and many people find the joy of bringing home a grown-up dog to be even greater than the fun of getting a puppy.

Papillon Rescue

One of the great opportunities for owning a Papillon and helping out a dog in need is Papillon rescue. The Papillon Club of America organizes a network of volunteers who foster and then find permanent placements for homeless Papillons. Although some of these dogs have special needs, many are healthy, friendly, little dogs whose human passed away or could otherwise no longer care for the

Busy families and single adults don't always have the time to take care of a Papillon pup. Consider adopting an adult Papillon instead.

Adopting an adult Papillon from a rescue organization is a great way of helping out a dog in need. Contact the Papillon Club of America for rescue organizations in your area.

If you are interested in showing your dog, your breeder will be able to help you select the right dog. Show dogs need to adhere to the breed standard.

dog. Rescue volunteers carefully screen prospective adopters, matching the right dog with the right household. For more information about Papillon rescue, go to the Papillon Club of America website (www.papillonclub.org) and click on "Rescue."

A rescue dog may or may not have AKC papers, depending on his life circumstances. Happily, the AKC has the Indefinite Listing Privilege (ILP) program. If you have a dog that is obviously a purebred and the dog has been spayed or neutered, you can apply to the AKC for an ILP number for your dog. This will allow you to compete in obedience, agility, rally obedience, tracking, and other AKC performance sports if you're interested.

Buying a Show Dog

You might be toying with the possibility of getting a show dog. Showing dogs can be an exciting, rewarding, and life-changing hobby. It can also be expensive.

If you decide you want to show your dog, first thing's first: Become a student of the breed; don't just leap into the purchase of a show dog because someone says the dog is show quality. Before considering purchasing a show dog you should do some of the following:

Study and begin to understand the breed standard. This is the blueprint for the breed so know what's in it. However, the breed standard has been compared to the Constitution–it's a relatively small document that is interpreted by judges. Knowing the standard backward and forward is just the beginning.

Go to dog shows. Watch the dogs and the judging. Try to understand what makes one dog win more often than the others. Pay close attention to the "specials"—the champions who are shown with hopes of Group placements or Best-in-Show wins.

Get to know the show exhibitors in your area. Talk with them about what it's like to show dogs. Find someone you respect, and talk about the possibility of finding the right show dog for you.

Show breeders aren't going to sell their very best show prospects to the first stranger who comes along, and they aren't likely to sell a potential champion with no strings attached. Expect an agreement, preferably in writing, that details what the breeder expects of you. It will probably require you to show your dog at a specific minimum number of shows. It may require you to hire a professional handler if you aren't successful at showing the dog yourself.

The contract is likely to include requirements about breeding the dog, and the breeder may have rights to one or more future puppies from your dog. Your breeder may want to maintain co-ownership of the dog. Look at the agreement closely, and think long and hard before you sign it.

Showing dogs is the thrill of a lifetime for many Papillon lovers, but it's something to go into with open eyes, and only with people you respect and trust.

CARING for Your Papillon

Getting the perfect Papillon is just the beginning. This isn't like a fairy tale that ends, "And they lived happily ever after." Your relationship with your dog, like any other relationship, depends on what you put into it.

GETTING A GOOD START

For the rest of your life, you'll remember the day you brought home your Papillon. Let's just hope it's a joyful memory, instead of the recollection of a disaster.

Plan ahead to make sure that your Papillon's first days and weeks with you go smoothly and happily. From this good start, you'll enjoy a lifetime of companionship.

Before you bring your puppy home, stock up on supplies. To do any job right, you need the right tools. Owning a Papillon is no different. Here's the essential equipment for any Papillon and how to use it with your new pet.

Your Papillon needs to get used to wearing a collar and leash. Let him walk around freely with the collar and leash on so that he becomes accustomed to them.

Collar and Leash

Finding an appropriately sized collar and leash can be harder than you think. A tiny little dog with a big collar and a huge leash looks pretty bedraggled, and he certainly won't enjoy a walk as much as a dog with a light collar and small leash.

Major pet supply companies and catalogues have a growing number of small collars. Be sure to get a dog collar and not a cat collar, since cat collars usually have a break-away mechanism for a cat's safety. The last thing you want your Papillon's collar to do is to release your dog. Your little Papillon doesn't need a "choke" collar or a prong collar—a small buckle collar or a collar that snaps on will be just perfect.

Finding slender leashes with tiny, lightweight hooks is a challenge. You might check out cat leashes, which tend to be lighter than dog leashes. The best solution is to go to a dog show; the wide variety of vendors there will have all kinds of tiny leashes for toy dogs.

Identification

Get an identification tag for your Papillon's collar, with your name and phone number on it. Papillons can have an unfortunate

Your Papillon needs to be wearing his collar when outside. His collar should have his ID tags in case he gets lost.

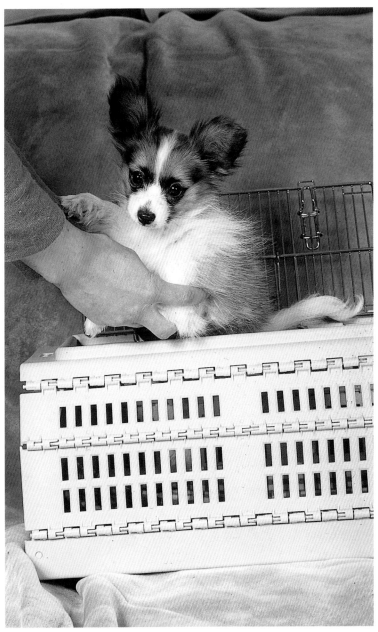

A crate is an essential training tool. The Nylabone® Fold-Away Pet Carrier makes crate training easier and helps with potty training.

adventurous streak, and sometimes will bolt out the door in search of fun, not thinking about the consequences until they're far from home. This is especially likely to happen with an adolescent dog or a dog who has just been placed in a new home. Your dog's identification tag on his collar can be his ticket home in case of an emergency.

Food and Water Bowls

Make sure the food and water bowls are small enough for your Papillon to use comfortably. A Papillon could take a swim in the bowl that a full-sized dog enjoys. Your dog should have fresh, clean water available at all times.

A Crate

Before you mumble to yourself that you'll never put your dog in "doggie prison," think again. A Papillon doesn't see a crate as a cage or a jail, he views his crate as his den. It's a nice, quiet spot to hang out when things get too rambunctious for a little guy. A crate is a home away from home when you travel with your dog. Crates, from the point of view of a Papillon, are a wonderful invention.

When your dog is outside, be sure he's in a fenced-in area or an exeercise pen. Never leave your dog unsupervised outdoors.

You want your Papillon to enjoy his crate and view it as his personal room. Here are some tips for successfully crate training your Pap. If space is a concern, buy a Nylabone® Fold-Away Pet Carrier. It will save you room by folding down for easy storage.

Purchase a sturdy crate that is large enough for the dog to stand, sit, turn around, and lie down in.

Teach your dog to enjoy his crate. Start out by simply placing a dog treat in the crate and letting the dog eat the treat. Later, close the crate door briefly. Over the course of a couple of days, gradually work the dog up to staying in the crate for two-hour increments.

Always reinforce the fact that the crate is a great place. Locate it where the dog feels like part of the family, such as the living room or your bedroom. Feed your dog his meals in his crate.

Never put your dog in his crate for punishment. The crate is a happy place, not the canine equivalent of Siberia.

When you put the dog in his crate or let him out of the crate, be matter-of-fact. You aren't rescuing him from prison. He's just leaving his room and coming into the rest of the house.

Other Containment

In addition to using a crate, some Papillon owners contain their dogs in exercise pens or in a gated-off area of the house. Baby gates, available from pet supply stores (and sometimes less expensively from baby departments of discount stores) can provide a barrier at the door of the kitchen or bathroom, giving a small dog a little bit of freedom while still keeping him out of harm's way. Exercise pens are small, flexible, portable wire fences that can be placed anywhere in your home.

Leave your Papillon in an enclosed area whenever you aren't there to supervise him. Letting a dog, especially a puppy, roam freely through the house is a sure recipe for housetraining problems and needlessly exposes him to untold household hazards.

Before relying on the security of a baby gate or exercise pen, however, watch your dog carefully. Many Papillons are gifted little climbers and pull themselves up over baby gates and exercise pens. If your Papillon is a climber, you'll have to rig a top to your exercise pen or leave your dog in his crate, because a Papillon can seriously injure himself catapulting off the top of an exercise pen or baby gate.

A variety of chew toys, such as those made by Nylabone®, will help to keep your Papillon busy when you can't keep an eye on him. They also make great rewards when training.

TOYS

Puppies need toys that will help with the teething process, and Papillons love to play with toys throughout their lifetimes. Different Papillons like different types of toys. Some love plush toys twice their size, others enjoy the tiny tennis balls available at pet supply stores, and some like plastic squeaky toys. Try out a variety of toys. Nylabone® Chew Toys are safe alternatives. As your dog gets older, let him select his own toys when you go to the pet supply store. Your Papillon will tell you with a smile and a wag of his tail which toy he wants to bring home.

Be careful with any toys that have eyes, threads, or other pieces that can come loose and get stuck in a Papillon's throat. Throw away any stuffing or squeakers if the dog tears the toy apart. Swallowing one of these objects can be a medical emergency.

Puppy-Proofing Your Home

Papillons are remarkably inventive dogs. However, a Papillon's clever intelligence can sometimes get him into serious trouble. Papillons climb, they pounce on anything that's dropped, they open doors, and they worm their way into spaces that are too small for a gnat. Before you bring your puppy home, be sure that electrical cords are covered (you can get cord covers at computer stores and at many variety stores). Make sure any dangerous household chemicals are stored in a top cabinet—or preferably somewhere such as the garage where your little Papillon will never go.

Have a supply of Bitter Apple (or similar product) from the pet supply store. This is a harmless spray with an unpleasant taste. Spray it on anything the dog is likely to decide to chew.

There are two products that don't belong in any Papillon home: slug bait and traditional, sweet-tasting antifreeze. Slug bait is a horrible, lethal concoction that causes the deaths of many dogs every year. Antifreeze is just as bad. A *half teaspoon* of antifreeze can kill an adult Papillon! There are now a number of brands of antifreeze on the market that have a bitter taste and have a less lethal set of ingredients.

Puppy-proofing your home is not an easy task. Put up baby gates to restrict the dog's movement when you are not around.

You need to decide ahead of time where your Papillon is going to sleep. You may decide to get a dog bed for him or to just let him sleep in his crate.

THE HOMECOMING

Now that you've done all the preparation, it's time to bring home your new puppy or adult Papillon. If it's at all possible, try to take at least a week off from work to help your new four-footed family member adjust to life in his new home.

Your Papillon's trip home should be in a safe, comfy crate filled with some nice bedding and a toy or two. Have multiple towels with you, so you can replace his bedding if he happens to get car sick on the way home.

Be sure the dog eliminates before he gets into the car. If the drive home is a long one, plan to make a potty stop or two along the way. However, if you're traveling with a puppy that hasn't had his complete series of vaccinations, don't let him walk on grass that has been used by strange dogs. This may expose him to deadly parvo and distemper viruses that his system can't handle.

Plan to spend a couple of quiet days with your new puppy or adult dog. Let him explore your home at his own pace. Don't force yourself on him, and don't invite all your friends over for a look at

Some Pap owners allow their dogs to sleep on their beds with them.

your new wonder dog. Let him have the time to get acquainted with you and to adjust to his new home. Some Papillons are wagging their tails happily from the first five minutes; others are more cautious and will adjust more slowly. Your bond of trust with your dog will be strengthened by letting him absorb his new life in his own way. Give him time to rest and relax. Don't poke at him when he's sleeping or try to wake him up to get him to play.

Decide ahead of time where your Papillon is going to sleep. Because dogs are pack animals, they benefit from spending their sleeping time near us. Your Papillon will be a happier, more bonded pet if he sleeps in your room. Place his crate near your bed where he can see you, and let him know he's part of the family.

Frankly, most people sleep with their Papillons on their beds, whether they will admit it in public or not. It's not like these little dogs take up a lot of room. However, if your Papillon *ever* growls at you, snaps at you, or otherwise shows highly dominant behavior, he doesn't belong on your bed. Let him sleep in a crate by your bed, but don't give him the doggie social status of sleeping on the same level as you. If you aren't having any dominance problems, let your dog sleep wherever it's most comfortable for you and your family. Many Papillon lovers sleep better with their small flock of Papillons arranged in their spots around the bed.

SOCIALIZATION, SOCIALIZATION, SOCIALIZATION

You know the first three rules of real estate: location, location, location. Well, the first three rules of having a happy Papillon are socialization, socialization, socialization.

If you expose your Papillon to new people and places in the right way and at the right time, he'll be a confident, friendly, adaptable little dog. If you don't, he's likely to be frightened of strangers and strange places and may have unpredictable behaviors.

Much of your dog's ability to respond to the world depends on how well the breeder socialized your Papillon as a puppy. It's important for the dog to see a variety of people and experience different places (even if it's just going from room to room in the breeder's house and playing in the yard). The puppy should have received loving, gentle handling from a variety of people.

Although life is easiest when a puppy has been well-loved and well-socialized in those critical early weeks, don't despair if your dog didn't get an ideal start. You can do a lot to make up for it. They

Papillons need to socialize with other people and other animals. This Pap and his rabbit friend just love each other.

say that it's never too late for a person to have a happy childhood. Your loving, gentle, consistent socialization can help make up for any sad puppyhood your dog may have had.

On the flip side, great socialization by the breeder is only a start. You need to continue the good job that the breeder started. Socialization is a lifelong process.

Animal behaviorist and veterinarian Dr. Ian Dunbar says that, as a rule of thumb, a puppy needs to meet 100 people before he's 3 months of age.

Unfortunately, the critical time for socialization happens at the identical time that your puppy is receiving his immunization shots for such deadly diseases as distemper and parvo. Until he's immunized, your puppy can pick up some viruses when he romps through grass that's been contaminated by a sick dog.

You need to balance your Papillon puppy's absolute need for socialization with his critical need for safety. Make smart choices about where you expose your puppy. Avoid public parks, rest stops, and other places where you'll find dogs with unknown health and vaccination histories. On the other hand, it's a good idea to take your puppy to friends' homes who don't have dogs or whose dogs receive excellent veterinary care.

One of the advantages to Papillon ownership is the fact that Papillons are so small. If you're in a place, such as a pet supply store, where there may have been unvaccinated dogs, just carry your puppy.

If a puppy meets new people and new dogs, and he has a bad time, all he's learning is that people and other dogs are scary. It's the good experiences that make a dog social.

So, expose your pup to children—but nice ones. Don't make your puppy endure a child who is grabbing at his fur, running around, or screeching. Look for a quiet, polite child who will gently pet your Pap and give him a treat, or maybe play a little game of fetch.

Give your puppy a huge variety of people and experiences, including things such as umbrellas, people on skateboards, power tools, the beach, and cats. Carry treats with you and give the puppy praise and a tidbit when he explores the world. This teaches him that new experiences are a fun part of the life of a dog.

Watch for signs of stress in your puppy; a tail tucked under the rump, ears down, head down, or yawning. If you see stress, back off a distance and slow down. Gradually move closer, as your Papillon accepts the new experience.

The same rules of socialization apply to older dogs. If you have a rescue dog or a poorly socialized dog, start slowly and gently, as if he were a puppy. If you have a more confident, well-socialized adult, don't forget to keep taking him places and stimulating him.

PAPILLONS AND OTHER DOGS

Dogs need socialization with other dogs, and Papillons are no exception. Generally, the more experienced your Papillon is with social interaction, the less likely he is to be attacked by another dog, since he'll be accustomed to giving and receiving appropriate body language.

Seek out other small dogs for your Papillon to play with. This is especially important if he's a puppy, but Paps usually enjoy a happy romp with another dog throughout their lives. There are several informal groups that get together for Papillon Play Days, which is ideal socialization and recreation for your dog.

Papillon Play Days are a great way for your dog to socialize with other Papillons. It's also a great chance for their owners to discuss breed-related issues.

If there isn't a Papillon Play Day near you, think about creating one. There's nothing more fun than seeing a swarm of Papillons, running like a river, bowing, wagging, leaping, flying. Papillons are usually very low-aggression dogs, and 30 or more usually play for hours without incident. And if one doesn't play nicely, the owner just picks the dog up and holds him.

The second-best alternative is play dates with other small breeds. Little, friendly dogs like Toy Poodles, Pugs, and Maltese make good playmates. Beware of play with terriers, since many of these dogs were bred to kill game that is bigger than your dog!

Under no circumstances let your Papillon play with a dog that is substantially bigger than he is. Don't rely on someone else's assurance that his or her big dog won't hurt yours. Even a friendly, sweet dog can break your dog's delicate bones in play. It isn't worth the risk.

Papillons and Big Dogs

Take special care if you live with both mini-sized and maxi-sized canines. Make clear rules and keep them. Don't let the dogs take

The Papillon is friendly and gets along with most other dogs. Just remember to supervise all interactions with other dogs so that your dog doesn't get hurt.

each other's toys, and don't tolerate snapping or growling from either dog. A scene that would be a minor squabble between canine siblings can become a calamity when one dog is large and the other is small.

Even if your Papillon and your big bruiser are best buddies, don't leave them loose together when they're unsupervised. All it takes is a misplaced paw or an out-of-control skid when you're gone and you'll return home to tragedy.

Too many small dog owners think that it's funny or even admirable when their little dogs bark and charge at big dogs. It's not. The big dog is likely to respond to your dog's aggression with his own aggression, and your little Papillon will lose every time.

If it's not acceptable for a Rottweiler or a Doberman Pinscher to snarl, snap, and lunge at another dog, it's also not acceptable for your pint-sized Papillon to do so. Teach him to look at you and sit or heel quietly when he's around other dogs.

Safety is especially important when you're walking your Papillon. Teach your dog an emergency lift-up command. Another good safety strategy is to use a harness instead of a collar on your small dog so you can pull the dog up into the relative safety of your arms in an instant.

Think of it this way: Other people may have purchased their dogs for protection; Papillons have their people for protection.

Socializing with the Big Dogs

While you don't want your Papillon to play with big dogs, it's a good idea to socialize your dog around some safe, well-trained, well-controlled larger dogs. If your Papillon has had some good, safe experiences with a large dog, he's less likely to bark at one or panic near one.

If you have a friend with a highly trained dog or know a knowledgeable person, such as a dog trainer, see if you can set up a training session around the big dog. If the big dog has a *reliable* down-stay and is *never* aggressive, ask the big dog's owner to have her dog lie down. This will allow your Papillon to greet the big dog nose-to-nose and say hello. Practice basic obedience around the big dog so that your Papillon learns to relax and do his work in the presence of a big dog.

Just because a big dog and small dog can be friendly doesn't mean they should be friends. Don't let this turn into a play session with a big dog. This is just a time for peaceful co-existence.

Going out to a dog park might not be the best thing for your Papillon if there are a lot of large dogs there. Some cities have dog parks for small dogs only, which would be more appropriate and safe for your pet.

Dog Parks

Dog parks are a bad idea for a Papillon. Not only are they full of large dogs, it's easy for a pack mentality to form. When one of the dogs decides that your Papillon looks like a rabbit, all the dogs just may decide to pursue your pup.

A few cities have opened small dog parks. Depending on the dogs that come to that park, this can be a nice play opportunity for a bold, somewhat larger, well-socialized Papillon.

FEEDING YOUR PAPILLON

In today's nutrition-conscious world, everyone has an opinion on exactly what you should feed your Papillon. They will tell you if you don't follow their advice, you're being an irresponsible, uncaring dog owner. It can feel overwhelming. Remember that most Papillons live long, healthy lives and seem to thrive despite what we might do.

Before tackling the sometimes controversial subject of what to feed your Papillon, consider when, where, and how much to feed. This part's easy!

When to Feed

From the time a puppy is weaned from his mother's milk until he's three months old, he needs to be fed four times a day. From three to six months, feed three times daily. After age six months, feed twice a day. Meals should be spaced evenly throughout the day, but the last meal should be at least three hours before bedtime so you don't have nighttime housetraining problems.

When you bring your new Papillon home, continue to feed him the brand of dog food he was eating at the breeder's home. Make any food changes gradually.

Meals Versus Free-Feeding

Feed your Papillon regular meals—don't just leave a dish down for your dog to free-feed. This can be the most important

The number of feedings and the amount fed will vary as your Papillon gets older. Ask your veterinarian or breeder for help in setting up a feeding schedule.

Free-feeding, or leaving food out all day for your dog, may sound like a good idea, but it is advised to feed regular meals several times a day.

commitment you make to your little dog. Here are a few of the important reasons why feeding your Papillon regular meals is a good idea.

- You will know when your dog is sick. The fastest way to notice a health problem is when a dog eats less at his meals for a day or two. No matter how observant you are, you can't catch this as quickly if you free-feed. Noticing a dog or puppy is "off his feed" on the first day can make the difference between life and death with some diseases.
- You will have a better relationship with your dog. Our Papillons may not look like wolves, but they share their wolf ancestor's view of pack hierarchies. When your dog chooses when and where he eats, he assumes he's in charge of the house. When you give your dog regular meals, he assumes you're in charge of the house.
- The difference in his behavior when you switch from free-feeding to giving your dog meals can be almost magical. It can even help with problems like housetraining and nuisance barking, since it will make your dog more likely to listen to what you ask of him.

You can give your Papillon treats throughout the day, but remember that these treats should be nutritious and are a part of his daily food intake.

- Although most Papillons stay slender naturally, some have a tendency to overeat. Feeding your dog meals allows you to control your dog's weight.

The Amount to Feed

The portion size varies according to your Papillon's age, activity level, and metabolism. Ask your dog's breeder how much food the dog has been getting at each meal. If the dog starts to gain weight, slightly reduce the portions. If your dog begins looking too thin, slightly increase the portions.

Where to Feed

The best place to feed your dog is in his crate. This gives your dog a safe, quiet place to enjoy his meals. It also gives your dog a positive association with his crate, which is also important.

What to Feed

Feeding high-quality food to your Papillon is extremely important. Depending on your Papillon's size and metabolism, he may eat less than half a cup of food a day. Even a few mouthfuls a day of doggie "junk food" can have a serious impact on your dog's health. Feeding your dog the right food, in the right amounts, is one of the things that you can do to help ensure that he lives a long, healthy life.

This doesn't seem too complicated, until you find yourself trying to pick out dog food at a major pet supply store. You'll find yourself staring at more than 150 brands, varieties, and flavors of dog food. Add to this the advice that you'll receive from people; for example, you should cook your own food or you should only feed raw, natural ingredients, and it's enough to make you want to throw up your hands in frustration.

Once you break down the choices that are available to you, however, the right options for your Papillon will become a lot clearer, and you'll come to a solution that works for you and your pet.

Before we worry about areas in which knowledgeable people may disagree, let's talk about the area in which every one agrees— quality counts. The better the quality of ingredients that go into your Papillon's food, the better it will be for your dog.

Commercial Dog Foods

The vast majority of Papillon owners feed their dogs some form of commercial dog food.

The Association of American Feed Control Officials (AAFCO) sets standards that most pet foods meet, ensuring that the food contains the right mix of such things as protein, fats, and vitamins. Although these standards are a good place to start, they don't guarantee that the products used in the food will actually deliver those nutrients to your pet. In fact, one pet food company demonstrated that it's possible to meet the standards with a formula that included old shoe leather and crank case oil.

Papillons don't eat a lot of food, and there's no reason not to spend a little extra money and get a premium brand for your dog. These foods may not be available at grocery stores; look for them at pet supply stores or at your veterinarian's office. Before you buy, read the ingredients listed on the package. When you bring the package home, open it and smell the food. It should seem like a fresh biscuit, not musty or rancid.

Fresh, clean water is as important to your Papillon's health as nutritious food. Make sure he has plenty of water, especially on hot days.

Historically, most pet foods have added the chemical preservatives BHA, BHT, or ethoxyquin to extend a product's shelf life. These additives have been a bone of considerable contention. There is concern that these chemical preservatives can cause cancer.

There are natural alternatives to chemical preservatives. Because there is an alternative, why expose your Papillon to the possible dangers of food laced with chemical preservatives? Seeing consumers' preferences for naturally preserved food, even major pet food brands are increasingly switching to preserving their food with vitamin E (usually listed as "mixed tocopherols" on the label) rather than with chemicals.

Because Papillons don't eat a lot, and because natural preservatives don't last as long as chemical ones, keep a close eye (and a sharp nose) focused on your dog food packages. If your dog's food seems less fresh toward the end of the bag, go ahead and buy a fresh bag and discard the old one.

Not only are the preservatives getting more natural, but the other ingredients are also. There is a rapidly increasing number of brands of dog food that include only organically raised meat, vegetables, and grains. These are available at the growing number of dog health food stores, through mail order and online, and at some pet supply stores. In fact, some major health food grocery store chains now stock several brands of premium, all-natural dog food.

Kibble Versus Canned

If you're giving your Papillon commercial food, it's important to feed kibble rather than canned food. Our breed's major health problem is loss of teeth. Although feeding kibble by no means solves all the potential problems of Papillon tooth loss, it will help somewhat to keep tartar accumulation under control. Feeding a diet of soft food makes the dental problems worse.

Cooking Your Own

Given the benefit of fresh, healthy ingredients, lots of Papillon owners are cooking their own dog food. Although home-cooked food can be very beneficial for your dog, if you don't do it right, home cooking will do far more harm than good.

Dogs have different needs for the mix of carbohydrates, proteins, and fats in their diets than humans do. There are a number of doggie

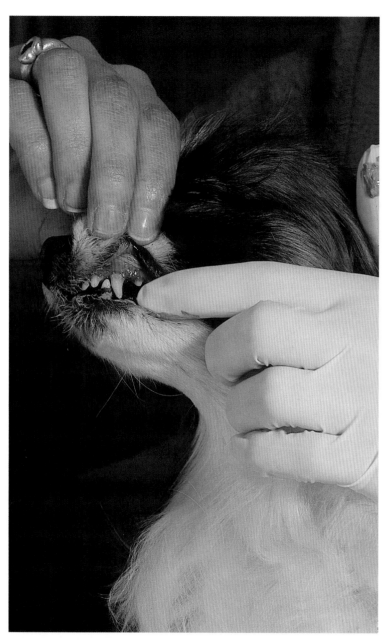

Many vets recommend hard kibble as part of a dog's nutritional needs. Not only is it healthy for your dog, but the texture can also help in keeping your dog's teeth clean.

cookbooks now available. Some of them have some wonderful recipes, but frankly, others are recipes for disaster and don't provide the necessary nutrients to keep your dog healthy.

Before you start to cook for your dog, get a diet from your veterinarian. When you look at homemade recipes for your dog, make sure that the balance of ingredients reflects the diet that your veterinarian gave you.

Raw Foods

In the past several years, a raw foods diet revolution has swept the dog fancy. Those who feed their dogs raw foods swear by the result. While skeptics worry about threats of salmonella and e-coli, those who advocate the diet respond that a dog's digestive tract is designed to handle raw meat.

It's extremely important to do research before putting your dog on this diet. Correctly done, this diet includes pulverized vegetables as well as enzymes. Feeding your dog raw meat alone will result in an undernourished, sick dog in short order.

A puppy with a top-quality diet radiates good health.

Papillons love treats and rewards when they are being trained. Just remember that all treats should be small and are a part of your Pap's daily food intake.

Several companies are now making frozen raw food diets, which you can purchase and keep frozen in your freezer. If you feed raw food, make sure that the food is fresh, bowls are washed carefully with soap and water, and that you use excellent hygiene.

The next few years should produce more information, which will tell us whether raw food diets are just a fad or a major revolution that will improve the health of dogs.

Whatever decision you make regarding your Papillon's food, keep a careful eye on him. Is his coat shiny and silky? Is his skin supple? Is he free of itching or dryness? Are his eyes free of watering and discharge? If your dog looks exceptionally healthy, you may not want to think about changing his diet. If he doesn't look as wonderful as he might, it's time to consider some of the alternatives that are available to you.

Treats

Dogs are healthiest when they're eating a well-balanced diet, whether it's a commercially prepared kibble, home-cooked meals, or a carefully planned and prepared raw foods regimen. Don't upset your dog's balanced diet with lots of needless treats.

Most obedience trainers train their Papillons with food as a reward. It's important to remember even in training that a tiny amount of food goes a long way in a little dog. Training rewards should be no larger than a pencil eraser. Use good quality treats, such as string cheese or cooked meat. Papillons also love veggies (tiny bits of carrots are a big favorite) and simple treats like an occasional oat cereal.

Remember, food rewards are for a job well done, not for begging at the table!

GROOMING Your Papillon

apillons are among the most naturally clean of all dog breeds. Many Papillons groom themselves like a cat, licking their paws and carefully washing their faces. Some Papillons even use their paws to clean out their own ears. Although watching a Papillon groom himself is fascinating, our dogs need our help. Regular combing, trimming, and bathing, combined with special care for your dog's teeth and nails, will ensure that your Papillon always looks and feels his best.

Happily, Papillons are basically "wash-and-wear" dogs. Although their coats are beautiful and their ear fringes can be dramatic, Papillons require less grooming than most long-haired breeds. Papillons don't need professional grooming.

In many dog breeds, the grooming for show dogs is so elaborate that the pets don't remotely resemble the show dogs. Papillons, on the other hand, need little grooming. With minimal effort, your dog's fur can look just as shiny and flashy as a Best in Show winner.

REGULAR BRUSHING

Brush your Papillon at least twice a week. It will keep him mat-free, is good for his circulation, and will improve his bond with you.

Although they can be expensive, a natural bristle brush is ideal for brushing your dog. The bristles are soft on a Papillon's sensitive skin, but they still penetrate through the coat. Be sure to pay special attention to your Papillon's culottes, under his tummy, and around his ears, all of which are places that mats are likely to start.

Grooming sessions should begin when your Papillon is still a pup. By beginning while he is young, he will become accustomed to the routine and enjoy being groomed.

To make your Papillon's coat look its best, spray a little water or grooming spray on your brush so that you aren't brushing a dry coat. (Brushing a dry coat causes your Papillon's hairs to break, leaving you with a shorter, less luxuriant coat.)

Once your Papillon is thoroughly brushed, gently pull a metal comb through his coat, making sure there aren't any tiny mats. Comb carefully and thoroughly around the base of your dog's ears, because this is the spot where most Papillons tend to get mats.

It's always sad to see people brushing and combing a Papillon too hard. You can see the little dog hunching inward and pulling away from the brush. Make brushing a gentle, happy, loving time together. Slow, patient, gentle brushing and combing will be a pleasure for your dog and it will create a loving bond between the two of you. Harsh, rapid strokes of a brush or comb with damage the bond.

Start brushing your Papillon from the day he comes home. If he's a four-month-old puppy with short hair, so much the better. He'll benefit from experiencing the sensation of brushing without you having to worry about tangles.

At about nine months of age, when your puppy's ear fringes are just beginning to grow in, comb the area around his fringes daily. At this point, there is inevitably a large mat that develops right at the base of the ear unless you are extremely vigilant about grooming your Papillon's ears.

When you're finished with your regular brushing, gently touch your dog all over—his muzzle, ear leather, neck, shoulders, body, legs, and feet. This light massage helps to reinforce the pleasurable sensation of grooming. It's also an important opportunity to check your dog for tumors, hot spots, lesions, or anything else that seems to be odd. This touching can lead to the early detection of many diseases and could save your Papillon's life.

Cleaning Ears

Check your Papillon's ears every time you brush him. Do they smell clean and fresh? Is there any accumulation of wax? If you see some wax, clean out your dog's ears with a ball of cotton. Don't stick a cotton swab into your dog's ears—a movement of his head could seriously harm your dog.

Papillons should be thoroughly brushed at least twice weekly. Always brush the coat in the direction that it naturally lies.

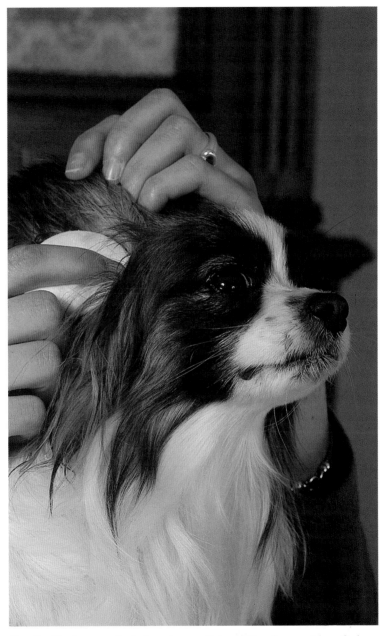

Your Papillon's ears need to be kept clean at all times. Wipe the ears with a soft, damp cloth to remove any dirt and wax buildup.

If your Papillon has an excessive amount of ear wax or an unpleasant odor in his ears, make an appointment with your veterinarian. It could be a sign of something that needs medical attention, such as an ear infection or ear mites. The dog could also need deep ear cleaning, which needs to be done by a veterinarian.

BATHING YOUR PAPILLON

Papillons are sweet-smelling dogs and have to be pretty grimy before they have any doggie odor. Their coats should be glossy, not dry or oily. Regular bathing is an important part of

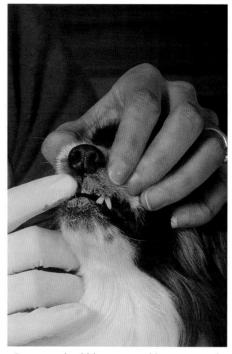

Grooming should be an enjoyable experience for you and your Papillon.

keeping your Papillon looking like the beloved pet he is, and it helps him to feel his best.

Purchase a gentle, hypoallergenic dog shampoo. You'll probably find a good brand at your veterinarian's office, at a local pet supply store, or at a dog show. Don't use people shampoo, which is formulated for a human's body chemistry.

Many Papillon owners also use cream rinse on their dogs. It makes their coats shinier and keeps their coats detangled during the drying process. There is usually a wide array of dog cream rinses at pet supply stores, and there is always a stunning array of choices at dog shows. Find a brand that works for your dog.

Papillons are small enough to bathe in the sink. Be sure to put a protective screen over the drain so your dog isn't putting his foot down the drain constantly. Place a towel or rubber mat on the bottom of the sink so your dog won't be scrambling to keep his footing on the sink's slick surface. A spray attachment to your sink

Regular baths keep your Papillon looking and feeling good. Dry your Papillon's coat thoroughly after bathing him. If it is a nice day, let him finish drying outside.

is an invaluable tool, since you're really giving your dog a shower, rather than a bath.

Always brush your Papillon before bathing him. Washing a matted dog will only make the mats tighter and harder to comb out.

Thoroughly rinse your Papillon with lukewarm water, making sure to get the thicker fur on his culottes, tummy, and neck soaked through. Apply the shampoo and cream rinse according to directions.

Rinse off the shampoo and cream rinse and then rinse your dog again. If you leave shampoo or cream rinse on his coat, his skin can become irritated and itchy.

Towel-dry your Papillon to get him as dry as possible and comb through his fur. Finish drying him with a blow dryer. It's a great luxury to have a specially designed dog hair dryer, which sits on a stand, keeping your hands free for grooming. However, your own hair dryer is very adequate for the job. Be sure the dryer is set on *low*. Keep your hand in front of the nozzle to dilute the flow of air and to make sure the temperature of the air coming from the dryer is cool enough for your Papillon's sensitive skin.

TRIMMING

Papillons require minimal trimming. There are a couple of areas that benefit from a little bit of scissoring, however. Remember to always use a small pair of scissors with a rounded tip.

Trimming Feet

Many Papillons have "fuzzy feet," with hair around their paws that makes them look like they're wearing bedroom slippers. This is unattractive and can be uncomfortable for your dog. Trimming the hair underneath his foot will ensure that your Papillon has good traction and that he won't pick up nasty things such as bubble gum on his feet. For an attractive appearance, trim around the sides of your dog's paws. Some people leave the hair on the toes longer, as it adds to your Papillon's hare foot appearance.

The Papillon coat requires little trimming. You may decide, however, to trim your Papillon's coat around the feet and the hocks.

Trimming the Hocks

Trim the long, feathery hairs on your dog's back leg, from his foot up to his hock (the heel bone). This will add to your dog's dainty, elegant appearance.

CLIPPING NAILS

Your dog will be in painful misery if you let his nails grow too long. If you can hear his nails clicking when he walks, it means that with every step he takes, his nails are pushing against his feet.

Most Papillons have nails that are easy to trim. Position your dog on your lap or on a table. Hold the dog's paw gently in your hand and snip off the very tip of the nail. For most Paps, cat nail clippers work wonderfully: they're small and, for most people, easier to control that the guillotine-style dog nail clippers.

Just trim the very tips of the nails; you don't want to hit the quick (the nerve that runs through your dog's nail). If your dog's nails are long, trim them back once a week, a little at a time. Eventually, the quick inside your dog's nails will retreat, and your Papillon will soon enjoy the comfortable feeling that comes with well-trimmed nails.

Don't forget to trim the nails on your Papillon's dewclaws, if he has them. (Dewclaws are the toes located on your dog's ankle.) These nails grow very quickly, because they don't ever receive any wear. They can grow into your dog's skin. Regularly checking and trimming declaws isn't hard to do, and it's very important.

If you work slowly and carefully, there is no reason to ever nick the quick and make your dog bleed. If this does happen, just hold the end of your Papillon's nail against the tip of your finger, and the bleeding will quickly stop.

If your dog pulls his feet away, get him accustomed to you touching his feet without the nail clipper. Just hold his paw gently, and if he pulls away, move your hand with it, so you're never pulling at his foot. Eventually, he'll give up and let you just hold his foot. Tell him he's a good dog and repeat the exercise each day. Over time, begin to rub his paw gently and massage between his toes. If he's comfortable having his feet rubbed and held, he won't be upset when you trim his toenails.

If you have a very wiggly puppy, or if the concept of cutting your dog's nails just seems too much for you, don't hesitate to take your Papillon to a local dog groomer to have his nails clipped. It's a very

All dogs need to have their nails trimmed from time to time. Use a clipper or a grinder to trim the nail to an appropriate length.

quick, inexpensive process. While you're there, ask the groomer to show you how to trim the nails yourself.

DENTAL CARE

Dental problems are the most persistent health concerns that many Papillons face. Papillons have a full set of teeth in a tiny muzzle, and it's sadly common for Papillons to lose many of those teeth at a young age. Even worse, the buildup of bacteria in a dog's mouth can lead to kidney, liver, and heart problems.

Perhaps the most important thing you can do for your Papillon's health and comfort is to take the best possible care of his teeth.

Brush your Papillon's teeth at least twice a week. Don't use human toothpaste, which will upset a dog's tummy. Your veterinarian can supply you with specially formulated dog toothpaste—most dogs prefer poultry-flavored toothpaste! This type of toothpaste has enzymes that will help break down plaque. Apply the dog toothpaste with a gauze pad, a small rubber brush that attaches to your finger, a cat toothbrush, or a child's toothbrush. It can be hard to reach your Papillon's back teeth, but it's important to do so if you want to keep your dog's mouth free of disease.

Encourage your Papillon to chew on safe toys. Many Papillons love fuzzy or furry toys. These toys can act much like dental floss,

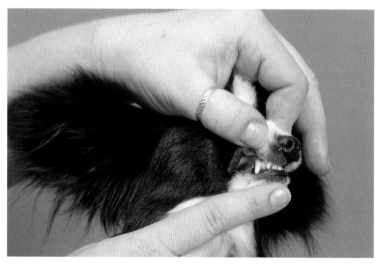

Your Papillon needs to have his teeth checked regularly. If you notice plaque buildup, contact your veterinarian to have them cleaned.

Safe chew toys, such as those made by Nylabone®, can help control tartar and plaque buildup.

reducing the build-up of plaque. Nylabones® are safe toys that can help eliminate plaque build-up.

When it's necessary, have your Papillon's teeth cleaned by your veterinarian. Just like people, the accumulation of plaque varies widely among individuals. Some Papillons need teeth cleaning every six months, others may be able to go a few years between cleanings. When you take your Papillon in for routine visits, always be sure that your veterinarian takes a close look at your Papillon's teeth and determines whether it's time for a dental cleaning.

TRAINING YOUR PAPILLON TO ACCEPT GROOMING

You may be looking at your Papillon and thinking, "This is not going to happen. There is no way that this wriggly, bossy, insistent little dog is going to let me brush his teeth, clip his toenails, or trim his feet. I give up!"

Papillons are intelligent, highly trainable dogs. Spend some time with your dog and soon he'll be a delight to groom. How? By pairing grooming behaviors with happy, tail-wagging times for your pet.

Teach "Lift-Up"

Lots of Paps don't really like to be picked up. It's scary and unpleasant—it probably feels to them like it would to us if a helicopter came and snatched us off the ground. However, you can teach your dog to tolerate it and maybe even learn to like it.

Every day, pick up your Papillon, with a cue word such as "Lift up!" and then reward him with a "Good boy" and a treat. Soon your dog will welcome this and may ask to be lifted up.

Teach Body Parts

Once your dog is accustomed to being lifted up, begin gently touch body parts, starting with just one. Teach the dog the name of the body part. For example, touch an ear, say "Good ear!" in a soft, happy voice, give the dog a treat, and put him back on the floor. After doing that a few days, touch his ear, ("Good ear") and also his toes ("Good toes!" and a treat). Gradually add body parts, giving treats and making this a happy time.

This process will make grooming infinitely easier. It will also make visits to the veterinarian much less traumatic for both you and your dog. Dogs are able to accept and cooperate with you much better when they know what is going to happen.

Tellington Touch

If your dog is still stiff or panicky when you groom him, consider learning Tellington Touch, also called T-Touch. This gentle technique uses specific circular motions on the surface of the skin. It's soothing, calming, and restorative. Regular T-Touch sessions will help your dog to enjoy being held and touched.

There are several books on the subject as well as certified T-Touch practitioners who live around the country who teach seminars in the technique or who can show you individually how to use the technique. For more information about T-Touch, check out the website of T-Touch creator Linda Tellington-Jones at www.tteam-ttouch.com.

Always remember that much of your dog's appearance comes from the inside, not the outside. A healthy, well-balanced diet, plenty of exercise, and weight control will all make your Papillon's coat shinier, eyes brighter, and attitude happier.

HOUSETRAINING and Training Your Papillon

Papillons are among the most trainable dogs on the planet. You can have a great time doing interesting activities and just plain having fun with your clever dog. If you're worried that training is about choke collars and force, you can relax. You don't need to use harsh methods on your Papillon and he'll actually learn better and faster with gentle methods.

Today, training is all about communication. The more you work with your Papillon, the closer, more bonded you will be. It's a fun, joyful, and loving process.

HOUSETRAINING YOUR PAPILLON

While some Papillons figure out the concept quickly and easily, others can be very difficult to housetrain. This is a typical problem in Toy dogs. In fact, housetraining problems are the most common reasons for small dog owners to return their dogs to the breeder.

Why? If you think about it, it's logical that small dogs are going to have more trouble than big dogs for a number of reasons.

Potty training will be much easier for your Papillon pup if you continually bring him back to the same spot to eliminate.

They have a difference sense of space. A small dog might pee in the corner and feel proud of himself. In his mind, he's gone away as far from his bed as a full-sized dog who's gone to the far end of the yard. Lots of small dogs have trouble grasping the concept of distance.

They have smaller systems. Papillons and other Toy breed puppies can take a long time for their systems to mature. A Papillon puppy may be six months or older before his system is mature enough to hold back from urinating or defecating right after meals, exercise, or sleep. Expect to continue to work on the fundamentals of housetraining well into your puppy's adolescence.

Their genetics may be different. Let's face it: if a Great Dane or Saint Bernard doesn't get the hang of housetraining pretty quickly, it's not likely to stay someone's pet for long. The odds are that dog will never, ever be bred. Because small accidents are so much less difficult to live with, small dogs that have housetraining problems have reproduced for generations—probably since small companion dogs first appeared in medieval castles. A Toy dog may not have the same strong instinct to ask to be let out that a big dog has.

Don't worry! With a little patience, and a lot of consistency and vigilance, your Papillon can become reliably housetrained.

How to Housetrain Your Papillon

Housetraining a Papillon takes time and patience. There are a number of different things that will make housetraining go as smoothly as possible.

1. Confine your dog! It's not fair to expect your puppy to understand housetraining if you give him free run of the whole house (or the entire living room). He needs to be confined to a space he understands.

2. Unless he's just eliminated, keep him confined to a small area, such as your kitchen or bathroom. When you want him to hang out with you, tie a 6-foot leash to your waist, so he doesn't have the room to make a mistake. (This also teaches him to stay near you—a great lesson for a companion dog!) When you leave the house, confine the puppy to a crate, an exercise pen, or the corner of an indestructible room.

3. Take your dog outside—don't just put him out the door. A Papillon or other toy-sized puppy is likely to get lonely, or become distracted. He's not likely to eliminate on his own. Go out there with him, and praise, praise, praise when he potties!

Familiarize yourself with the telltale signs that your Papillon needs to be taken outside to eliminate.

4. Teach your puppy a "permission to potty" command. When he
   potties, say "Good potty!" (or whatever word you choose) and
   reward him with pets and maybe even a treat. Eventually, when
   you say "Potty!" your dog will potty. This saves enormous
   amounts of time in your life and is a real help when you're
   traveling and you take your dog to unfamiliar surfaces.

   To make your job quicker and easier, and less troublesome for
you and your Pap, it helps to keep the following in mind.

   Never punish your dog for a mistake. It only adds to your
Papillon's anxiety and slows down the process.

   Think about your female Papillon's comfort! Because females
need to squat down to eliminate, a tall clump of grass that a large
dog would never notice is an insurmountable object to a toy-sized
female when she tries to urinate. Take her to a part of the yard that
doesn't have grass, such as a garden area. You might also have to
shovel snow to give her a usable spot.

   Watch for signals that your dog needs to go out. Some dogs never
get the idea of going to the door and asking to go out. They may
come and look at you, or they may circle or trot around restlessly. Learn to read your dog's way of telling you that he needs to potty.

   Note: Papillon males are notorious leg-lifters. Male dogs lift their legs and pee a small amount to mark territory. This is different from a dog who is pottying, which will be a noticeably larger amount of urine. A male dog can be otherwise perfectly housetrained but still mark. This is particularly a problem in houses with multiple male Papillons that have not been neutered.

Never scold or yell at your Papillon for not following a command. Simply put him in the last correct position and continue from there.

Puppies cannot control their bowels and bladders for too long. If you're leaving the house, make sure your puppy has newspaper or other absorbent materials available, since accidents do happen.

Have faith! Housetraining your Papillon can be a slow process, but one day the light will go on. Your dog can learn this!

Neutering your dog, especially when he's a puppy, can decrease this problem significantly. Confining the dog to a small space and tying the dog's leash to your waist also can help. Some people who have several intact males resort to putting belly bands (also called a cummerbunds) on their dogs. This is a strip of cloth with an absorbent pad to manage the problem.

TRAINING YOUR PAPILLON

Remember, training isn't just about teaching dogs to "sit" and "stay." It's about leadership. You can make your Papillon feel safer, more secure, and calmer if you let him know—in gentle, non-violent doggie language—that you're in charge.

It's important to be our dogs' leaders. If we aren't, bossy Papillons become unbearable; shy dogs become petrified. The biggest gift you can give to your dog—and to your relationship with him—is to be a kind, gentle, consistent leader.

If humans don't act like leaders, dogs become very stressed and anxious. They can't count on you. It makes everything harder for

Every dog has the right to be trained. Teach your Papillon exactly which behaviors are tolerated and which ones are not.

You and your dog should not be distracted during a training session. He should be focused on you and your commands the entire time.

the dog: dealing with people coming into the house, going to the vet, even the rituals of bedtime and dinner.

If you aren't a leader, bold Papillons will become the "little tyrants" that some call them. They're likely to become barkers and sometimes even growlers and nippers. Still, these dogs aren't feeling safe and secure. They know there's something wrong when the 7-pound dog is running the house. It's even worse for shy dogs, who can only feel secure with a strong leader that they feel will protect them.

You don't have to be violent or even raise your voice to be a leader. You just have to convey leadership in dog terms. Here's what to do every day.

Don't free-feed your dog. Give him two meals (three or four meals during puppyhood). In the wolf pack, the head wolf is in charge of food—so this tells your dog that you're in charge.

Require your dog to perform the sit, down, or to do a trick before he gets a treat or his dinner. If you're having dominance problems with him, require him to sit, down, or do a trick before you pet him.

You decide when the dog is allowed on the bed. Teach him "on" and "off" the bed. When you get in bed, tell him "off" and (if you want to sleep with him) tell him he can get back on. In the wolf pack, the head dog determines who sleeps where.

Tell him to "wait" at doorways. Go through in front of him.

Introduction to a Collar and Leash

Gradually introduce your puppy to his collar. Don't use a choke collar on your Papillon. They have slender necks, and a constriction of a choke collar can cause permanent damage to your dog's throat. A simple buckle or snap collar is great, or a harness also works well. Let him get used to the feel of this new thing around his neck. Once he's had his collar on for a few days, put on his leash. Let him lead the way, as you follow him where he wants to go. Once he's accustomed to the feel of the leash, show him a treat and have him come a few steps with you. Over time, he'll get used to following you on his leash.

Next, teach your dog to walk on a loose leash: You want to be able to go out in the world and have fun with your Papillon. Whether it's neighborhood walks, enjoying a trip to the beach, going on a vacation, or visiting with friends, it's important that your Papillon can walk happily—and calmly—on a loose leash. This is when you should teach your Papillon the "Let's Go" command.

The "Let's Go" command is all about learning to follow your lead on the leash. Once your dog is accustomed to his collar and leash, start going places. Say, "Let's go!" (or "walkies" or whatever word suits you) and start going. It's likely that your dog at some point will decide to leap to the end of the leash—ready to go in a different direction.

When this happens, instantly turn and say, "Let's go!" and start going the other direction. You might get a little dizzy at first, but your clever Papillon will soon learn that the only way for him to go the direction he wants to go is to keep the leash loose. Once he figures this out, walking your Papillon will be a joy.

Never, ever jerk your Papillon by his leash and collar. This can permanently damage his neck and back, and it will erode his trust in you. His time on a leash with you should be joyful and pleasant.

Training with Food?

Trainers used to tell students never to give food rewards. Science has proved that was bad advice. Dogs learn faster when they have a reward, just like people do a better job when they're paid.

Before going out, make sure your dog is wearing his leash. Never allow your Papillon to roam or run loose when out in public.

Praise and reward your Papillon for successfully completing a command. The positive reinforcement and the treat will make him want to continue to please you.

Remember, Papillon rewards shouldn't be big chunks of food—a tidbit the size of a pencil eraser is all you need. Also, not every reward needs to involve food. Give him toys, a scratch on the rump, or a happy moment of play for a job well done. Always, always praise him when he does it right.

To Click or Not to Click

In the last decade, clicker training has taken over the world. Trainers hold a little device that gives a distinct "click"—and click when the dog does a desired behavior. The clicker is always tied in with a reward so that distinct sound makes the dog joyful, knowing he's done something right and will be rewarded.

To teach a Papillon to respond to a clicker is easy. Click and give the dog a treat. Click and treat. Click and treat. At this point, your clever Papillon is well on his way to clicker training.

A great way to explore clicker training is with a kit that explains how to do simple tricks such as High Five, Spin, and Roll Over, or teach basic manners like Sit and Time For Bed. They're called Quick-Click kits and are available at your favorite pet retailer or by going to www.tfh.clickertraining.com.

While some people love clicker training and find it an epiphany in their training, others don't like having a clicker in one hand while they have treats, a leash, and a dog to keep track of.

The instructions in this chapter will work whether or not you're a clicker trainer. If you are a clicker trainer, "click" in the sections of this chapter where it says to say "Good dog."

Whether or not you click, it's important to help your dog understand that his good behavior makes you happy and that training is always fun, rewarding, and loving. Training is never a time to make a Papillon afraid or anxious.

Teaching "Watch Me"

This may be the most important lesson you teach your dog. A dog who is looking at you can't bark and lunge at another dog. It's physically impossible. A Papillon who is looking at you is more likely to learn what you are teaching him (just like kids in school are more likely to learn when they watch their teacher).

You can teach "Watch me" to a puppy or adult in a day of fun interaction. Here's how you do it.

It's never too early to begin training your Papillon. Good training ensures that he will become a well-mannered adult.

Teaching your Papillon a "watch me" command can help to control undesirable behavior. A dog that is watching you can't be distracted by another dog.

1. Hold a treat between your eyes and say, "Watch me." Your Papillon will stare at you—well, the treat—longingly.

2. Instantly say, "Good watch me!" and reward the dog with the treat.

3. After the dog is looking at you consistently, hold the treat in your hand (out of sight of the dog). Say, "Watch me." If he looks at your face, say, "Good watch me!" and reward him. If he looks at your hand, say, "Uh-uh, watch me." If he looks at your face, reward him. If he doesn't understand, hold the treat in front of your eyes again and remind him of what you want.

4. Over time, mix up holding treats in front of your eyes and having a treat in your hand until you eventually always have the treat in your hand.

5. Gradually require the dog to look at you for longer periods of time before giving the reward.

6. Practice "watch me" several times a day, always with a food reward!

Playing "catch" with food treats also rewards your dog for paying attention to you. Hold a treat just a couple of inches over his head and say, "catch!" If it drops to the ground, pick it up and try again. The only time your dog gets the treat is when he catches it in mid-air. Do this several times, and most Papillons will be catching mid-air in a matter of minutes. This game requires them to pay attention to you—and that's a good thing!

Teaching the Sit Command

The first thing that most dogs learn is a "sit." It's a wonderful command that keeps your bouncing Papillon in a stable, safe place.

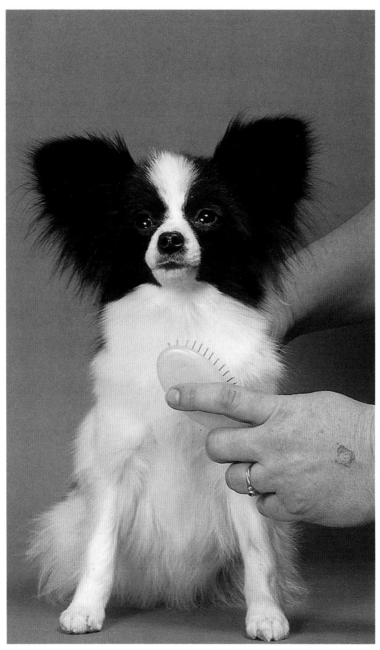

A good "sit" is helpful in daily life for convenience and safety.

To teach sit, first hold a treat in front of the dog's nose. Next, slowly pull the treat over the dog's head, between the dog's ears. Almost all dogs will naturally "rock" back into a sit. Say, "Good sit" and give the reward while the dog is in the sitting position.

If the dog doesn't automatically sit, gently tuck your finger just above his hocks to help him go into a "sit" position. If your dog is turning around, you might want to practice in a confined space such as on a chair. If he's going up on his back legs, you're holding the treat too high.

Don't *ever* push down on your Papillon's rear end to make him sit. It can damage his delicate hips and back. Don't ever pinch his kidneys (as some trainers show you), as this can potentially harm him internally.

Teaching the Come Command

The come command should be the most joyful, glorious, happy command your Papillon can hear. He needs to know that when he turns and runs to you, great and wonderful things will happen: treats, play, kisses, toys. When your Papillon is chasing a squirrel, and you call him, he needs to know that it's more fun to come running to you than to chase the squirrel. Yes, you have to be more interesting than a squirrel!

The sit command should be given to your Papillon at the beginning of each training session, because it is the foundation of all the other commands.

The down command is a difficult one for your dog to learn. The down position in the dog's pack is a sign of being submissive.

In order to do this, teach the come command in a way that he can't make a mistake. Start out with him on a long leash, so if he runs away, you can collect him. It helps to be very, very fun. Call him in a happy, high-pitched voice. Squat down and clap your hands or turn and run the other direction. Make yourself interesting and appealing.

When your dog comes to you, treat him and praise him for at least 15 seconds. Dogs want to know that you're excited that they came to you—so act like it! Remember, don't ever call your dog to you for punishment or something even mildly unpleasant. If you need to clip your dog's nails, go collect him—don't call him.

Use a magic word. If you've used the word "come" to mean something else, or if the dog does not respond to "come," use a word he will respond to. Use "here" or "front" or something cute and clever. Just don't use a word your dog has been ignoring for years.

Practice three times a day. Don't overdo this one, because you want to keep this a spontaneous, joyful communication between you and your dog.

Teaching the Lie Down Command

"Lie Down" is one of the most important commands you can teach your Papillon. If you need to keep him absolutely still and

Puppies learn the ropes of canine behavior from a parent or older dog. If your adult dog has good habits, they may be passed on to your pup.

under control, nothing is more effective than the down command.

It can be a little confusing for a dog who's already very close to the ground to figure out that you want him to lie down. This is especially true since Papillons spend so much of their lives airborne.

However, with a little patience and encouragement, your Papillon will be dropping into a "down" with enthusiasm. Here's how to do it.

The dog should be standing and relaxed. Take a treat and hold it between his front toes. He'll reach down for the treat and may drop in a "down" position.

If he doesn't drop, keep the treat on the floor, pushing it slightly toward his chest. He'll fold into position. As soon as he's in the down position, tell him, "Good down!" and give him the treat.

If he keeps backing up, try teaching this on a chair, so he can't keep backing up, and he'll lie down to get the treat.

Remember: If you use the word "down" to mean "off," use another word or phrase for "lie down." For example, say "lie down" or "drop." You can't have "down" mean get back on all four feet and also mean lie down on the floor.

Teaching the Stay Command

Before you start, here is an important concept: Always give your dog the reward while he's doing what you ask him to do. This is especially important for the stay command.

You may decide that taking your Papillon to an obedience class is the best way to train your dog. Check out local obedience classes to find the one that matches your style.

Most people teach their dogs the "un-stay." They say, "Stay! Stay there, boy. Good stay!" Finally, they release the dog and reward him. So what does the dog learn? That he gets rewarded when he gets up. If you reward a dog consistently while he stays still, then he'll learn to love that game.

Follow these steps to learn this life-saving command.

1. Be sure your dog knows and understands "sit" before you start. "Sit" and "stay" are two different commands.

2. After you tell your Papillon "sit," take a step back about six inches and gently say "Stay, good stay." Instantly, and while he is still sitting, reward him. He can't learn to sit for one minute until he's learned to sit for one second.

3. When he succeeds at a one-second sit-stay, expand the time to five seconds, then ten seconds, etc. If he consistently gets up after 15 seconds, for example, give him a 12-second "stay" and reward him. Help him succeed.

4. Chain together two or more "stays." Tell him, "stay" and reward after 10 seconds, then step back and tell him, "Stay" and reward him after another 15 seconds.

5. Work up gradually to longer and longer periods of time. Eventually, your Papillon will stay in a long sit or long down for several minutes without moving.

Finding an Obedience Class

You might want to take your Papillon to obedience class. The fun and discipline of going to class every week will be good for both of you. You're likely to find that your dog is the star of the class. You'll have a blast, if it's the right class for you and your Papillon.

Be extremely careful about choosing an obedience class for your Papillon. These are sensitive dogs who need positive training methods. They are also in real danger if a class is out of control and can be seriously hurt, or even killed, if a big, untrained dog decides to play with or harm your dog. Here are tips in finding a great class for you and your dog.

Go see the class. Don't take someone else's word that this is a great class—things that a Labrador owner would never notice can be a real hazard to your Papillon.

Look for safety. For example, some classes are taught in pet-supply stores. Are these classes safe or are they set up in a way that an owner who is shopping with his big, out of control dog just might plow over you?

Your Papillon must be taught that commands must be followed. Always be consistent in what you ask of your dog.

How does the trainer keep the dogs safe from each other? Is there plenty of room between dogs or are they piled up on top of each other? Does she emphasize to owners to keep dogs to themselves, or is it something of a free-for-all? Think about your Papillon and whether he'd be safe in the environment.

Does the trainer use positive methods? Jerking and pulling on leashes, yelling, even pushing dogs into a "sit" position aren't the right techniques to use on your small, sensitive dog.

Talk to the trainer. What experience does she have teaching toy-sized dogs? Ask her what safety provisions she can make for your dog in class.

Happily, in today's environment of positive dog training, it's easier than ever to find a class where your dog will be safe, happy, and have a chance to shine.

A word about puppy kindergarten: In the old days, dogs didn't go to obedience class until they were six months old. Now, many experts say that the most important class a dog can have is puppy kindergarten, which usually welcomes puppies over 12 weeks of age.

Puppies learn basic skills, such as walking calmly on a leash, coming when called, and sitting on command. More importantly, the puppies learn social skills. They find out that being held and petted by strangers is fun. Some classes even arrange for children to come so that dogs have experience with kids.

Praise your Papillon for doing things right. Affection in the form of hugs, kind words, or a new Nylabone® will reinforce the positive behavior while preventing problems from arising.

Problem behavior should not be tolerated. Excessive barking, nipping, and growling aren't cute.

Puppy kindergarten also has the doggie equivalent of recess, where the pups engage in the serious business of puppy play. This is where you need to be a vigilant protector of your Papillon. It's great that your dog will have the chance to meet and play with other dogs, but don't let your dog wrestle and play with a big dog. You're asking for trouble.

Introductions should be slow and gentle, and play should be with dogs that are appropriately matched in size and temperament. It's important that your Papillon isn't mugged by an aggressive dog or else the puppy learns he can't trust other dogs. If you and the trainer are vigilant then your puppy can enjoy the experience.

PROBLEM BEHAVIORS

Papillons that Bark

This is a breed that can bark—and bark, and bark, and bark. Happily, Papillons are also very trainable. Here are some tips to get that barking under control.

- Acknowledge what your dog is telling you. Papillons know they hear things we don't. Like any sensible watch dog, your dog will want to tell you what's going on. If you ignore your dog or just tell him to be quiet, he may decide that you don't understand his message. He's likely to bark louder and more insistently.

- Instead of yelling at him to shut up, acknowledge what he's telling you. Go with him to the window and say, "I see the squirrel, thanks for letting me know." When your dog is barking, just saying, "Thanks for letting me know" will usually end the cycle, because your dog will know that you heard what he had to say.
- Teach him to whisper. Your Papillon can't bark unless he breathes in first. As he's taking that breath, say, "Good whisper!" and give him a treat if one's handy. Papillons are clever little creatures, and within minutes your Papillon will be coming up to you doing silent barks to get your attention. Silent barks are good. Noisy barks are incredibly irritating. Reward the silent barks.

The Anti-Cuddler

Not all Papillons like to be held, despite the fact they fit so well on a human lap. If your Papillon isn't a cuddler, you can do some things to make him enjoy human touch more.

Hold him gently and restrain him in your arms until he relaxes into your hold. Then tell him in a quiet voice what a good boy he is, give him a treat, and let him go. Practicing gentle restraint will help accustom your Papillon to touching.

Door Dashing

Papillons can be adventurous, and they are fast. Too many Papillons dash through doors, which can be deadly. Drivers don't see these tiny, fast dogs dash into the street. Some Papillons have run out the door and never been found.

Don't trust your Papillon around doors. A combination of training and vigilance is your best defense against this worrisome habit.

- Practice the wait command at the door. With your dog's leash on, practice "Wait" at your doorway. Open the door, say, "wait" and give the dog a treat. Reinforce the wait command every time you go outside, so at least your dog will hesitate before he thinks of crossing a threshold.
- Practice the come command from the outside in. With your dog on a leash, have him outside, and open the door from the inside. Call to him, and when he comes back inside, give him big treats and praise.

Once your Papillon has mastered the basic commands, you may proceed to advanced training and trick training.

Shyness in Papillons is usually a sign of poor socialization when the dog was just a puppy. Gentle training methods can help make your dog bolder.

• Manage the front door. Keep a baby gate across your entrance hall. Don't give your Papillon the chance to dash through the door. Don't ever, ever trust your Papillon around open doors—not for a minute.

Shyness

Although most Papillons are bold and outgoing, there are enough shy Papillons to warrant special mention. Most Papillons are gentle, fairly submissive dogs, and some are a little bit high-strung. It's not hard for those same genes to create a shy dog. Although shy Papillons occur even when the puppies are well-socialized and loved by their breeder, shyness is epidemic among puppies with poor socialization.

If you have a shy Papillon, gentle, loving, non-violent training is a key to helping him learn to be more bold. Take your dog places and do things in small doses to help him build up his confidence. That shy little Papillon can blossom into a great pet.

GO DO SOMETHING FUN!

You have the great fortune to have an exceptionally clever dog. Use that intelligence and energy to strengthen the bond between you and your dog. Go out and have some fun. The following are activities where Papillons excel.

Conformation

Conformation showing is the oldest dog show sport. This type of showing is based on the dog's appearance—that is his structure, movement, and attitude. When considering this type of showing, you need to be aware of the breed standard and be able to evaluate your dog compared to that standard. The breeder of your puppy or other experienced breeders would be good sources for such an evaluation. Puppies can go through lots of changes over a period of time. Many puppies start out as promising hopefuls and then after maturing may be disappointing as show candidates. Even so, this should not deter them from being excellent pets.

Conformation training classes are usually offered by the local kennel or obedience clubs. These are excellent places for training puppies. The puppy should be able to walk on a lead before entering such a class. Proper ring procedure and technique for posing (stacking) the dog will be demonstrated, as well as gaiting the dog. Generally, certain patterns are used in the ring, such as the triangle or the "L." Conformation class will give your youngster the opportunity to socialize with different breeds of dog and humans, too.

Obedience

Papillons, with their intelligence and desire to please, are fabulous obedience dogs. Take a beginner class—and then learn about competition classes. Your Papillon will love it. With today's non-violent, motivational methods, obedience training is as enjoyable for your Papillon as it is for you.

The AKC acknowledged obedience around 1936, and it has changed tremendously even though many of the exercises are basically the same. Today, obedience competition is just that—very competitive. Even so, it is possible for every obedience exhibitor to come home a winner (by earning qualifying scores), even though he/she may not earn a placement in the class.

Most of the obedience titles are awarded after earning three qualifying scores (legs) in the appropriate class under three different judges. These classes offer a perfect score of 200, which is extremely rare. Each of the class exercises has its own point value. A leg is earned after receiving a score of at least 170 and at least 50 percent of the points available in each exercise.

Obedience matches (AKC-sanctioned, fun, and show and go) are often available. Usually, they are sponsored by the local obedience clubs. When preparing an obedience dog for a title, you will find matches very helpful. Fun matches and show and go matches are more lenient in allowing you to talk to and help your dog in the ring. This type of training is usually very necessary for the Open and Utility classes. AKC-sanctioned obedience matches do not allow corrections in the ring since they must abide by the AKC obedience regulations booklet. If you are interested in showing in obedience, you should contact the AKC for a copy of *Obedience Regulations.*

Agility

Agility dogs fly through a course, leaping over hurdles, running across elevated catwalks and A-frames, and scooting through above-ground tunnels. You'll notice this is exactly what your Papillon does in your living room. These little dogs excel at this active, enjoyable sport, so sign up for a class.

Agility was first introduced by John Varley at the Crufts Dog Show in England in February 1978, but Peter Meanwell, competitor and judge, actually developed the idea. It was officially recognized in the early '80s. Agility is extremely popular in England and Canada and is America's most popular dog sport. The AKC acknowledged agility in August 1994. Dogs must be at least 12 months of age to be entered. It is a fascinating sport that the dog, handler, and spectators enjoy to the utmost. Agility is a spectator sport! The dog performs off lead. The handler either runs with his

Agility is the most popular dog sport in the US. Papillons have been known to excel at agility.

Dog sports are a great way for you to spend time with your Papillon.

dog or positions himself on the course. He then directs his dog with verbal and hand signals over a timed course, over or through a variety of obstacles, including a time out or pause. One of the main drawbacks to agility is finding a place to train. The obstacles take up a lot of space, and it is very time consuming to put up and take down courses.

The AKC, UKC (United Kennel Club), United States Dog Agility Association (USDAA), and the North American Dog Agility Council (NADAC) all hold agility trials throughout the country. Advanced titles require the dog to negotiate more obstacles and go faster than beginning-level work.

The AKC's top agility title is the coveted MACH—Master Agility Champion. These dogs really seem to move at the speed of sound—mach speeds! There are several Papillons who have earned the coveted MACH award.

Flyball

This relay race sport is sweeping America. A dog runs over hurdles, hits a box that throws out a tennis ball, and returns over the hurdles.

The height of the hurdles is determined by the size of the smallest dog on the team, so every flyball team is looking for a small, athletic dog that's built for speed. This sounds like a job for a Papillon.

Canine Freestyle

Do you wanna dance? The growing sport of canine freestyle—dancing with dogs—already has some Papillon stars. So get out and do that old-time rock n' rollover!

Animal-Assisted Therapy

Certified therapy dogs are welcome in nursing homes, hospitals, hospices, and other places where the healing power of dogs can make a profound difference in people's lives. Papillons, with their clever tricks, friendly natures, and love of people can make ideal therapy dogs. Anyone who volunteers for this worthwhile activity will tell you that the joy of watching sick or lonely people light up at the interaction with a Papillon is thrilling. You and your dog can make a difference in your community.

The activities you do with your Papillon are limited only by your imagination. Is someone teaching herding classes in your community? Many Papillons have an intense herding instinct and love to spend an afternoon herding ducks around a pasture.

Terrier clubs that teach "go-to-ground" techniques for ratting often welcome Papillons. Several Papillons have participated for exhibition only at earthdog events, successfully making their way through going through a tunnel to find a cage of rats. (Because the rats are caged, neither dog nor rodent can get hurt.) Many Papillons are also tracking dogs.

Find an activity, and just do it. Both you and your Papillon will be better for it, and the bond between the two of you will grow exponentially.

CANINE GOOD CITIZEN®

The AKC sponsors a program to encourage dog owners to train their dogs. Local clubs perform the pass/fail tests, and dogs that pass are awarded a Canine Good Citizen® Certificate. Proof of vaccination is required at the time of participation. The test includes:

1. Accepting a friendly stranger.
2. Sitting politely for petting.
3. Appearance and grooming.

Training your Papillon for the Canine Good Citizen® Test will ensure that he has good manners and will be welcomed anywhere.

4. Walking on a loose leash.
5. Walking through a crowd.
6. Sit and down on command/staying in place.
7. Come when called.
8. Reaction to another dog.
9. Reactions to distractions.
10. Supervised separation.

These exercises are a good test of a well-mannered dog that will reflect positively on your Papillon's owner and on the breed.

RESOURCES

The Papillon Club of America provides information on rescue, breed history, the "Pap Talk" monthly magazine, and other issues of interest to the breed. On the Web at www.papillonclub.org.

The American Kennel Club publishes *Events*, a monthly magazine that is part of the *Gazette*, their official journal for the sport of purebred dogs. The *Events* section lists upcoming shows and the secretary or superintendent for them. The majority of the conformation shows in the US are overseen by licensed superintendents. Generally, the entry closing date is approximately two-and-a-half weeks before the actual show. Point shows are fairly expensive, while the match shows cost about one-third of the point show entry fee. Match shows usually take entries the day of the show, but some are pre-entry. The best way to find match show information is through your local kennel club. Upon asking, the AKC can provide you with a list of superintendents, and you can write and ask to be put on their mailing lists. Find out more at www.akc.org.

HEALTH CARE

Happily, Papillons are among the healthiest and longest-lived breeds. Although there are some special health issues to consider, most Papillons live well into their teen years and are vigorous and energetic throughout their lives. Still, there are some issues to think about and some precautions to take to make sure that you and your Papillon enjoy the longest, healthiest time together.

THE VETERINARIAN

After you, there is no more important person in your Papillon's life than his veterinarian. It's important to find a veterinarian who is skilled, will take the time to examine your dog closely, and will communicate clearly with you.

FINDING A VETERINARIAN

There are lots of great sources for veterinary referrals. Your breeder, if local, may recommend her veterinarian. Friends and family members can also recommend veterinarians who have treated their dogs.

Wherever you get your referral, check out the veterinarian before you take your dog there. After all, the best veterinarian for your friend's Pit Bull might not be the perfect veterinarian for your Papillon. We also all have different personalities: The vet that your friend finds efficient might strike you as curt.

As long as you make an appointment ahead of time, the veterinary staff should be proud to show you their facilities. The entire clinic should be gleaming in its cleanliness. Veterinarians and other staff should show genuine fondness for animals, talking with them and touching them soothingly. They should be glad to answer your questions.

It's a good idea to interview your prospective veterinarian. This isn't an insult to the veterinarian—it's your job to find the right fit for you and your dog.

Here are some questions to ask when you visit your prospective veterinarian:

• How many Papillons or other toy dogs do you regularly treat?

Even healthy dogs need to periodically be examined by a veterinarian. Your vet will notice something is wrong if he knows what your Pap is like when in good health.

There is an art to caring for a toy dog that veterinarians who routinely work on larger animals may not develop.

- What kind of anesthesia do you use when you perform surgery? Papillons can be sensitive to anesthesia. Your veterinarian should be using one of the modern gas anesthesia, such as Isoflurane, which are far safer than old-fashioned intravenous anesthesia.
- Are you active in local or national veterinary associations? This is the best place for veterinarians to keep current on the latest developments in veterinary medicine.
- What arrangements are available if you're not here? Some veterinarians are on-call on off-hours. Increasingly, emergency veterinary clinics are available to take animals when other veterinary offices are closed.
- What kind of monitoring equipment do you have during surgery? Dogs are put under anesthesia frequently, for everything from spaying or neutering to teeth cleaning to X-rays. You want to be sure that the veterinarian has continuous monitoring for heart functions and other vital functions.
- Are you certified by the American Animal Hospital Association (AAHA)? Trained consultants regularly visit these veterinary hospitals to ensure compliance with AAHA's standards for services and facilities. Think of it as the "Good Housekeeping Seal of Approval" for veterinary offices. Although there are good veterinary hospitals that don't choose to participate in this program, certification is an indication that the clinic is committed to quality veterinary care.
- Do you have certified veterinary technicians on staff? Some veterinarians save money by having untrained veterinary assistants helping during surgery. The best veterinarians use certified veterinary technicians. These trained professionals complete a two-year, rigorous training program that is equivalent to college nursing training. Your pet is safer if your veterinarian is using the skills of a trained technician during surgery rather than an untrained assistant. Having a high-quality staff is a sign of a high-quality veterinarian.
- How long have the veterinarians on the staff worked here? Constant turnover in key staff is a warning sign that this clinic isn't a happy place. Of course, young veterinarians often eventually leave a clinic to start their own practices, so not all turnover is bad. Still, if most of the veterinarians have worked in a practice for just a year or two, ask why.

Ask other dog owners, especially other Papillon owners, for recommendations when selecting a vet. A vet who knows a lot about small dog breeds will be able to meet your dog's needs better.

- How long is a typical appointment? Some veterinarians schedule clients for every ten minutes, some for every half hour.

Keep in mind that the best veterinarian in the world won't do your pet much good if he or she doesn't communicate well. If the veterinarian can't speak effectively with you in an office visit, think how difficult that communication will be during a medical emergency or through the course of a long illness.

Remember, too, that the best veterinarian usually isn't the least expensive veterinarian. The most sophisticated equipment, the most qualified staff, on-going training—none of it's cheap. But when your Papillon is sick and needs help, you'll want to know in your heart that he's receiving the very best care available.

Many veterinary clinics have a number of veterinarians who practice at the facility. Select one as your primary veterinarian and ask for that veterinarian when you are making non-emergency appointments for your Papillon. Your dog will benefit from having one veterinarian who becomes familiar with him and can notice subtle changes over time.

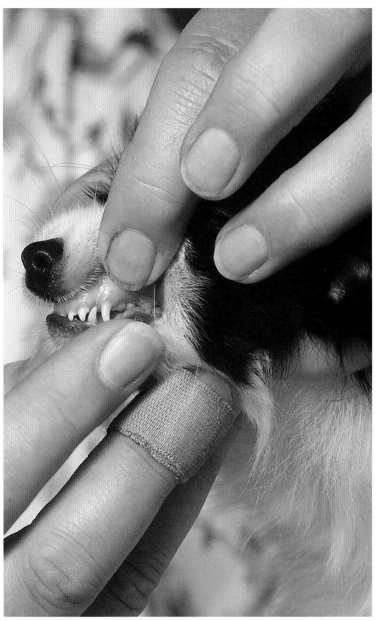

Your Papillon's teeth should be examined periodically. If you notice excessive tartar and plaque buildup, visit your veterinarian to have the dog's teeth professionally cleaned.

The Well-Pet Visit

Within 48 hours of bringing your new Papillon home, bring him to your veterinarian for a well-pet visit. Even if your dog doesn't have any shots due, it's important for your veterinarian to give him a comprehensive medical examination right away.

Your veterinarian will listen to your new dog's heart and lungs, palpitate his tummy, and look for abnormalities in the your dog's eyes. He or she will inspect teeth and gums and look for swelling in your dog's glands. Your veterinarian will want you to bring in a stool sample to check for worms. If there is a health problem with your new dog, a thorough veterinary exam will likely spot it.

A well-pet exam is a great time to see if this is really the right veterinarian for you. Especially for little dogs, the hubbub and newness of a veterinarian's office can be intimidating. Look for a veterinarian who holds your Papillon gently and talks to him. You can ask the veterinarian to give your puppy treats so that the puppy thinks the veterinarian is a fun and wonderful human being. Your dog's happy rapport with your veterinarian will go a long way to making shots, spaying or neutering, and other necessary veterinary procedures during her lifetime far less traumatic.

To maintain his good health, your Papillon should be immunized against contagious diseases by your veterinarian.

Your Papillon can pick up diseases from other dogs, so be careful when out for your daily walk or when visiting neighbors with dogs.

A note of caution at the vet's office: Remember, the veterinarian's office is a place where people bring their sick dogs. While veterinarians clean and disinfect their offices carefully, it's a good idea to hold your dog on your lap in the waiting area, especially if your puppy hasn't had his complete vaccinations yet.

There are many diseases that can cause your dog serious illness—canine distemper used to rage through kennels, shelters, and neighborhoods, and parvo killed countless puppies and adult dogs. It's important for your Papillon's health to get his vaccinations according to the protocol that you and your veterinarian agree upon. However, just what that protocol looks like is under serious discussion, and recommendations are undergoing change.

Puppy Shots

There is no controversy about the basics: All puppies need core immunizations. A puppy's mother's milk gives him immunity from most diseases for the first several weeks of his life. After that time, vaccinations give your puppy his own immunity.

Puppies are given a series of vaccinations, between the ages of six weeks and four months. Although many people assume that these shots gradually build up a puppy's immunity, this is not the case.

Accidents do happen, and unfortunately for a small dog like the Papillon, an accident can cause serious injury. Keep an eye on him when he's outside.

A puppy who still has temporary immunity from her mother's milk won't receive immunity from a vaccination. The problem is that it's impossible to know exactly when the mother's temporary immunity will wear off, so the puppy vaccines are repeated until the age of four months.

Vaccine Controversies

During the last few years, there has been a lot of controversy about the benefits versus the risks of various vaccines. Every vaccine has the potential to harm a dog. Some dogs can have a specific, even deadly, reaction to a vaccine. There is also evidence that over-vaccination actually harms the dog's overall immune system.

Remember, there is universal agreement that puppy vaccines are necessary and that the benefit of immunity far outweighs the risk of adverse reactions. Members of the veterinary community are taking steps to decrease the risk of adverse reactions while keeping your dog safe from deadly diseases.

It's increasingly recognized that vaccines aren't "one size fits all" protocols. Many vaccines come in modified live versions and in killed versions. Depending on the size, age, and general health of

A well-groomed dog is a happy dog. Regular grooming sessions will keep your Papillon looking and feeling his best.

the dog, your veterinarian will choose whether to give a live or killed version of the vaccine.

Many veterinarians believe that not all vaccine brands are of equal quality. Bulk vaccines are cheaper, but most veterinarians agree that single-shot packages provide better quality control and less chance of adverse side effects.

Depending on the size, age, and health of your Papillon, your veterinarian may space out vaccines rather than giving them in combination form.

There is growing discussion over which vaccines need annual boosters. Research is being conducted to determine the length of time for which each vaccine actually provides immunity. Talk with your veterinarian about what he or she recommends.

It's universally agreed that puppies should receive their core vaccines for rabies, parvovirus, distemper, hepatitis, and parainfluenza. All puppies should receive these shots; the frequency of adult booster shots should be determined by you and your veterinarian.

There are vaccines for other diseases, including leptospirosis, coronavirus, bordatella, and Lyme disease. Discuss the prevalence of these diseases in your community and your dog's lifestyle (for example whether you travel a lot, go to a lot of public parks, go to dog shows, or board your dog) with your veterinarian to determine whether any of these vaccines are appropriate for your Papillon.

The choices about which diseases to vaccinate against and how often to give boosters are important ones for the well-being of your Papillon. A dedicated, knowledgeable veterinarian who keeps up on the latest research about vaccine protocols is the very best defense against these frightening diseases. Ask your veterinarian about what vaccines he or she recommends, and why each one is included or excluded.

GIVING MEDICATION

You're likely to get some prescription medicine for your dog from time to time. It's helpful to teach your Papillon to take medicine without complaint.

Sometimes medicine can be put inside a treat and your dog will never notice. However, Papillons are clever dogs and usually figure this trick out pretty quickly. Sometimes sick dogs soon refuse to eat, since they're convinced that their food is laced with pills.

Your Papillon will occasionally require medication. Follow your veterinarian's instructions for administering the proper dosage.

If your dog is going to be on medication for an extended time, teach him that taking pills is part of life. Pop the pill down your dog's throat and stroke his throat until he swallows. Tell him that he's wonderful and give him a treat approved by your veterinarian. Soon your smart little dog will willingly take the pill, knowing that a treat will be forthcoming right afterward.

SPECIAL MEDICAL PROBLEMS FACED BY PAPILLONS

We are very lucky that Papillons are generally extremely healthy dogs and are usually active and vital well into their old age. However, there are a few health problems of which all Papillons-lovers should be aware.

Broken Bones

One of the top health problems in Papillons isn't a disease; it's the fact that these little dogs are breakable. This problem is compounded by the fact that Papillons seem to think that they can fly.

Sometimes surgery is needed to correct a problem or injury. This little Papillon will need some time to mend before he's back to his happy, carefree self.

Don't let your Papillon fling himself off of tables or off the back of the couch, especially if he is a puppy or a very fine-boned dog. Be very careful when you pick him up — hold him carefully so that he doesn't wriggle loose. Watch your puppy at all times and seek first-rate medical attention right away if he seems to have injured his leg.

Luxating Patellas
The kneecap in your dog's rear leg is attached by a groove in the bone. With tiny bones, it can be easy for the kneecap to pop out. This slipping of the kneecap is a common problem in all toy breeds. This condition can range from a slight "trick knee" that won't affect your dog's quality of life to a serious, painful condition that requires skilled surgery.

Watch for signs of limping or hopping. If you suspect a problem, talk with your veterinarian right away.

Progressive Retinal Atrophy (PRA)
Progressive retinal atrophy (PRA) causes blindness. All breeding stock should be screened and certified as clear by the Canine Eye

Spaying or neutering your Papillon can help correct some problem behaviors. It can also help your dog live a longer, healthier life.

Registry Foundation (CERF), indicating they are free of PRA and other eye abnormalities. Don't buy a puppy's whose parents haven't been determined to be free of PRA and registered with CERF.

Teeth

Dental problems are common in small breeds. If you think about it for a moment, it only makes sense. A millimeter pocket in the gum of a human—or a Labrador Retriever—is a small dental problem. In a tiny Papillon mouth, that pocket might lead to an extraction. Dental hygiene isn't just cosmetic. Accumulation of tartar, and the resulting bacteria in the mouth, contributes to other health problems, including heart, liver, and kidney problems.

Be sure to clean your Papillon's teeth regularly and take him for dental visits to your veterinarian. If you see tartar accumulation, or if your Papillon is experiencing some doggie breath, don't delay treatment. It will only make the problem worse.

Reverse Sneezing

Reverse sneezing is not a serious problem, but often scares a first-time Papillon owner to death. Papillons, especially when under some stress, will sometimes snort and gasp for breath. No one knows the cause of reverse sneezing. If it happens to your Papillon, gently hold your hand on your dog's muzzle or open her mouth with your fingers so he'll breathe through his mouth for a moment instead of through his nose. This should end the episode; no veterinary attention is required, unless the dog is struggling for breath—which means that the condition is something other than this small quirk.

Spaying and Neutering

Unless you plan to breed for the show ring, it's important to spay or neuter your pet Papillon. Here are some good reasons why.

Your dog will live longer. Breast, ovarian and testicular cancer are leading killers among dogs. The American Kennel Club Canine Health Foundation reports that the incidence of mammary tumors in female dogs is almost three times higher than it is in human women, and most canine mammary tumors are malignant. A female dog who hasn't been spayed by age 2 has a 50 times a greater risk of mammary tumors than a dog who has been spayed before she comes into her first heat cycle.

Examine your Papillon carefully for scrapes and bruises when returning in from playtime. Look for burrs or twigs that may become stuck in the pads of the paws.

Cancer isn't the only health risk. Male dogs who have not been neutered are much more likely to roam and to face the dangers of cars, other animals, and fights. Unspayed females can develop pyometra, a painful and dangerous—sometimes fatal—uterine infection.

Your carpets will thank you. Papillon males are notorious leg-lifters. Dogs that are neutered as puppies are the least likely to mark their territory. Even later neutering can help your carpets: About 25 percent of dogs stop almost all of their territorial marking after neutering, and about 60 percent reduce their marking behavior by more than half.

Having puppies is a bad idea unless you're financially and emotionally committed. Nowadays, some Papillons fetch a large sales price, so it's tempting to envision a fat profit from the sale of little dogs. The reality is very different.

Papillons have small litters—averaging only about two pups. Even a healthy female with a normal pregnancy can rack up medical expenses, including the cost of checkups (which may include ultrasounds and blood tests), testing for progressive retinal atrophy, and a stud fee, among other expenses. To make matters worse, sometimes Papillons run into complications during pregnancy or delivery, and some Papillon births are by Caesarian section. Sadly, some puppies die, even with the best of care and attention.

In the "old days" people wanted to teach their children about the miracle of birth, so they'd have a litter of puppies. Today, we know it's better to teach children lessons of compassion and responsibility—so teach your children the value of spaying and neutering and supporting responsible rescue organizations.

If you're considering becoming a breeder, don't rush into the decision. The future of the breed is in the hands of breeders. Purchase breeding stock from the very best lines in terms of temperament, health, and appearance. Go to seminars and read the dozens of books on the subject. Develop mentors in the breed, so that you're benefiting from the experience of people who know the breed well.

Put breed health as your top priority. Have all your dogs screened for PRA, and don't breed a dog who has luxating patellas or whose family tree has a history of the problem. Don't forget to factor in the time of socializing puppies.

Only breed if you are committed to protecting and preserving the well-being of this wonderful breed. People who breed with those values in mind, of course, seldom make a profit on a litter.

WHEN TO SEE THE VETERINARIAN

If you're worried that your Papillon isn't feeling well, take him to the veterinarian right away. An illness that may lay a large dog low for a few days can be fatal to a small dog. No one knows your dog as well as you do. If you notice a subtle difference in his energy level, the sparkle in his eye, the shininess of his coat, or the fluctuation of his weight, have it checked out.

Take your Papillon into the veterinarian *immediately* if you see any of the following symptoms:

- Vomiting, especially if it lasts for more than 24 hours. Violent, repeated vomiting should be treated right away.
- Diarrhea that has lasted more than 48 hours; bloody diarrhea should be treated right away.
- A dog that is straining to defecate but can't produce a bowel movement should be seen right away.

Your Papillon needs you more than ever as he gets older. The mature dog may need extra care and attention to stay healthy.

- Signs of seizure.
- Shortness of breath.
- Excessive thirst.

GERIATRIC CARE

Papillons are energetic and vital at an age when many breeds are old and frail. Even though your Papillon has the look and energy of a young dog—despite a few gray hairs—don't forget to keep a special eye on your senior dog.

When your dog turns eight, have a talk with your veterinarian about suggestions he or she might have to maintain your Pap's good health for many years to come. Your veterinarian might want to run some extra blood tests each year, and after a point might suggest that you bring your dog in every six months instead of once a year. These steps are important, because many illnesses are treatable or easily manageable if they're caught early, but can cause irreparable damage to your dog's vital systems if they are left untreated.

However, with the right care, and a little luck, your Papillon will have a good chance of living to be 14 or older. There are many people who have had Paps who have lived 16 or 17 healthy years; a few Papillons make it past age 20.

Oh, and the oldest dog to win Best in Show at Westminster in the 127-year history of the show? Ch. Loteki Supernatural Being, who was still in the prime of his life at age eight and a half when he beat the big dogs at Madison Square Garden in 1999.

IDENTIFICATION and Finding the Lost Dog

There are several ways of identifying your dog. The old standby is a collar with dog license, rabies, and ID tags. Unfortunately, collars have a way of being separated from dogs and tags fall off. Still, collars and tags are your first line of defense in bring your dog home. If they stay intact and on the dog, they are the quickest form of identification.

For several years, owners have been tattooing their dogs. Some tattoos use a number with a registry. Herein lies the problem, because there are several registries to check. If you wish to tattoo your dog, use your social security number. Humane shelters have the means to trace it. It is usually done on the inside of the rear thigh. The area is first shaved and numbed. There is minimal discomfort, although some dogs do not like the buzzing sound. Occasionally, tattooing is not legible and needs to be redone.

The newest method of identification is microchipping. The microchip is a computer chip that is no larger than a grain of rice.

Tattooing and microchipping are great methods of identifying your Papillon if he should ever become lost. Your dog should also wear his collar and ID tags at all times.

Make sure your backyard is escape-proof and always supervise your dog when he's outside. It's easy for these little dogs to escape through a small hole.

The veterinarian implants it by injection between the shoulder blades. The dog feels minimal discomfort. If your dog is lost and picked up by the humane society, they can trace you by scanning the microchip, which has its own code. Most microchip scanners are friendly to other brands of microchips and their registries. The microchip comes with a dog tag saying that the dog is microchipped. It is the safest way of identifying your dog.

FINDING THE LOST DOG

Most people would agree that there would be little worse than losing your dog. Responsible pet owners rarely lose their dogs. They do not let their dogs run free because they don't want harm to come to them. Not only that, but in most, if not all, states there is a leash law.

Beware of fenced-in yards. They can be a hazard. Dogs find ways to escape either over or under fences. Another fast exit may be through the gate that perhaps someone left unlocked.

Below is a list that will hopefully be of help to you if you lose your pet. Remember, don't give up, keep looking. Your dog is worth your efforts.

Make sure you have a clear, recent photo of your dog in case he becomes lost.

1. Contact your neighbors and put flyers with a photo on it in their mailboxes. Information you should include would be the dog's name, breed, sex, color, age, source of identification, when your dog was last seen and where, and your name and phone numbers. It may be helpful to say that the dog needs medical care. Offer a *reward*.

2. Check all local shelters daily. It is also possible for your dog to be picked up away from home and end up in an out-of-the-way shelter. Check these, too. Go in person. It is not enough to call. Most shelters are limited on the time they can hold dogs before they are put up for adoption or euthanized. There is the possibility that your dog will not make it to the shelter for several days. He could have been wandering or someone may have tried to keep him.

3. Notify all local veterinarians. Call and send flyers.

4. Call your breeder. Frequently, breeders are contacted when one of their breed is found.

5. Contact the rescue group for your breed.

6. Contact local schools—children may have seen your dog.

7. Post flyers at the schools, groceries, gas stations, convenience stores, veterinary clinics, groomers, and any other places that will allow them.

8. Advertise in the newspaper.

9. Advertise on the radio.

TRAVELING with Your Papillon

The earlier you start traveling with your new puppy or dog, the better. He needs to become accustomed to traveling. However, some dogs are nervous riders and become carsick easily. It is helpful if he starts any trip with an empty stomach. Do not despair, as it will go better if you continue taking him with you on short, fun rides. How would you feel if every time you rode in the car you stopped at the doctor's office for an injection? You would soon dread that nasty car. Older dogs that tend to get carsick may have more of a problem adjusting to traveling. Those dogs that are having serious problems may benefit from medication prescribed by the veterinarian.

Give your dog a chance to relieve himself before getting into the car. If your dog tends to get carsick, line his crate with a fresh towel. Replace the towel if he gets sick. Also, bring along some wipes to clean up the dog, if it becomes necessary.

Have a supply of chew toys available in your Papillon's crate so that he doesn't get bored when traveling.

You love your Papillon, and certainly would never consider letting him ride in the back of a pickup, where he might lose his footing and fall to the street. Your Papillon is undoubtedly part of the family, and rides in the safety and security of your car. Unfortunately, your dog might be a lot less safe than you think. Here are some things to consider:

- You Papillon can leap out an open window in a flash—even a window that's open just a crack. All it takes is the sight of a cat, a dog, or a bird. And if your poor pooch flies out the window when you're driving at 55 miles an hour, he doesn't stand a chance. Drive with the windows up if you animal is loose in the car. Better yet, make sure he rides in the safety of a crate.

- Airbags can be deadly. You probably know that a deployed airbag will easily injure—and maybe kill—a baby. It can do the same thing to your small Papillon. All small animals should ride in the back seat, just like an infant.

- Crates are the key to safety. The best bet is to keep your Papillon in a comfy crate, such as the Nylabone® Fold-Away Pet Carrier. If you have to slam on your breaks, or if you get in a fender-bender, you won't need to worry about your pet. The Nylabone® Fold-Away Pet Carrier is excellent for most dogs, but if your dog gets carsick, you may want to experiment with other types of crates. Some dogs do better with wire crates, which allow more air flow, while others do better with hard plastic crates which block out the view of moving scenery.

Safety doesn't stop when the car is parked. Don't ever leave your dog alone in a parked car on a sunny day. Even if the temperature is a comfortable 70 degrees outside, it can climb to a deadly level in a matter of minutes inside. Don't leave a leash on your dog if he's in the car, since too many owners have learned the sad way that a dog can hang himself in the excitement of waiting for your return. In some states, it is against the law to leave a dog in a car unattended.

Don't leave your dog in an unlocked car for even a minute. There are people who will try to steal your adorable little friend—and an unlocked car or a car with the windows open is almost an engraved invitation for a thief.

One of the joys of Papillons is the fact that they're portable. Instead of leaving the dog in the car, tuck him under your arm, or let him walk proudly with you where ever you go. It will make both of you happier!

Traveling with your Pap should always be fun as well as safe. In the car, your dog should be in a crate, such as the Nylabone® Fold-Away Pet Carrier.

TRIPS

Perhaps you are taking a trip. Give consideration to what is best for your dog—traveling with you or boarding. Another consideration for you when traveling with your dog is medical problems that may arise and little inconveniences, such as exposure to external parasites. Some areas of the country are quite flea infested. Be sure to treat your pet before you leave, under your veterinarian's supervision, with a topical flea treatment such as Advantage or Frontline. This is even a good idea when staying in motels. Quite possibly you are not the only occupants of the room.

Many motels and even hotels do allow canine guests, even some very first-class ones. One of the best sites is www.petswelcome.com for numerous and varied listings across the country and around the world. Once you've targeted a destination, always call ahead to any motel that you may be considering and double check that they accept pets. Sometimes it is necessary to pay a deposit against room damage. The management may feel reassured if you mention that your dog will be crated. If you do travel with your dog, take along plenty of baggies so that you can clean up after him. When we all do our share in cleaning up, we make it possible for motels to continue accepting our pets. As a matter of fact, you should practice cleaning up everywhere you take your dog.

Depending on where your are traveling, you may need an up-to-date health certificate issued by your veterinarian. It is good policy to take along your dog's medical information, which would include the

Some hotels and motels allow dogs. Call ahead of time to double check that they accept pets.

Professional pet sitters are available who will watch your dog in the comfort of your own home. If you are uncomfortable with a stranger watching your dog, ask a reliable friend to dog sit for you.

name, address, and phone number of your veterinarian, vaccination record, rabies certificate, and any medication he is taking.

AIR TRAVEL

When traveling by air, you need to contact the airlines to check their policy. Usually, you have to make arrangements up to a couple of weeks in advance when traveling with your dog. The airlines require your dog to travel in an airline-approved crate. If your dog is not accustomed to a crate, it is a good idea to get him acclimated to it before your trip.

Your Papillon will fit into a soft-sided dog carrier that you can bring on a flight as carry-on luggage. If you've crate-trained your dog and have introduced him to his airline carrier, he'll acclimate

If you can't take your Pap with you when you travel, you may have to leave him in a boarding kennel. Inspect the facilities and ask about any special requirements before leaving your dog anywhere.

to going on a plane just as he learned to ride in a car. Lots of Papillons have been frequent flyers, and time spent with you in the cabin is much less traumatic and less potentially dangerous than going by cargo. The day of the actual trip you should withhold water about 1 hour ahead of departure and food for about 12 hours.

While traveling with your pet in the cabin is usually easy, there are many more things to consider if your dog needs to travel as cargo. The airlines generally have temperature restrictions that do not allow pets to travel if it is either too cold or too hot. Frequently, these restrictions are based on the temperatures at the departure and arrival airports. It's best to inquire about a health certificate. These usually need to be issued within ten days of departure. You should arrange for nonstop, direct flights, and if a commuter plane is involved, check to see if it will carry dogs. Some don't.

The Humane Society of the United States has put together a tip sheet for airline traveling. You can receive a copy by sending a self-addressed, stamped envelope to:

The Humane Society of the United States
Tip Sheet
2100 L Street NW
Washington, DC 20037.

Regulations differ for traveling outside of the country and are sometimes changed without notice. Well in advance of your trip you need to write or call the appropriate consulate or agricultural

Traveling with your Papillon can be fun. Make sure you both get plenty of rest so you can enjoy your trip together.

department for instructions. Some countries have lengthy quarantines (six months), and many differ in their rabies vaccination requirements. For instance, it may have to be given at least 30 days ahead of your departure.

Do make sure your dog is wearing proper identification including your name, phone number, and city. You never know when you might be in an accident and separated from your dog, or your dog could be frightened and somehow manage to escape and run away.

Another suggestion would be to carry in-case-of-emergency instructions. These would include the address and phone number of a relative or friend, your veterinarian's name, address, and phone number, and your dog's medical information.

BOARDING KENNELS

Perhaps you have decided that you need to board your dog. Your veterinarian can recommend a good boarding facility or possibly a pet sitter that will come to your house. It is customary for boarding kennels to ask for proof of vaccination for distemper, parvo, and rabies. Most also require a bordatella vaccine within six months of boarding. Since it's possible that there may be dogs with fleas at the kennel, discuss flea treatment with your veterinarian before your trip, with a topical flea treatment such as Advantage or Frontline. Ask the kennel what kinds of activities your dog can expect. Some provide playtime with staff or other small dogs, grooming, or walks. Facilities usually charge extra for these amenities, but they can be worth it.

For more information on pet sitting, contact NAPPS:
National Association of Professional Pet Sitters
17000 Commerce Parkway
Suite C
Mt. Laurel, NJ 08054
Some pet clinics have technicians that pet sit and that board clinic patients in their homes. This may be an alternative for you. Ask your veterinarian if they have an employee that can help you. There is a definite advantage to having a technician care for your dog, especially if he is on medication or is a senior citizen.

You can write to the ASPCA for a copy of *Traveling With Your Pet:*
ASPCA
Education Department
424 E. 92nd Street
New York, NY 10128

RESOURCES

Papillon Club of America
Corresponding Secretary: Carol Morris
www.papillonclub.org

American Kennel Club
Headquarters:
260 Madison Avenue
New York, NY 10016

Operations Center:
5580 Centerview Drive
Raleigh, NC 27606-3390

Customer Services:
Phone: (919) 233-9767
Fax: (919) 816-3627
www.akc.org

The Kennel Club
1 Clarges Street
London
W1J 8AB
Phone: 087 0606 6750
Fax: 020 7518 1058
www.the-kennel-club.org.uk

The Canadian Kennel Club
89 Skyway Avenue
Suite 100
Etobicoke, Ontario, Canada
M9W 6R4
Order Desk & Membership: 1-800-250-8040
Fax: (416) 675-6506
www.ckc.ca

The United Kennel Club, Inc.
100 E. Kilgore Road
Kalamazoo, MI 49002-5584
(616) 343-9020
www.ukcdogs.com

INDEX